Preface

Excel is one of the true marvels of modern civilization! An over-statement? Perhaps. But if you have struggled with any of Excel's predecessors, you will readily come to appreciate its sophistication and elegance. In all probability, however, you have not yet utilized Excel to the utmost. Like any state-of-the-art product, Excel has capabilities and intricacies that are not readily evident from perusing the instruction manual. Indeed, it would take months of experimentation to discover all of Excel's extraordinary features, convenient shortcuts, and hidden charms.

It is the purpose of this book to allow you to forgo the months of experimentation and to quickly unleash a full measure of Excel's abilities, focusing them toward the goal of a smooth-running small business. A glance through the second part of the Contents will reveal some specific business applications. If you are so inclined or if you are in a hurry, you can put Excel to work immediately by skipping the chapters in the first part and going directly to the applications. Follow the simple directions there for entering the formulas, and within a few minutes Excel will be balancing your books, projecting your profits, or amortizing your mortgage, to name but a few examples.

If you prefer to construct your own custom-designed applications worksheets, you will definitely want to start at the beginning of the book and get to know Excel thoroughly. The chapters in the first part expand on concepts in the instruction manual, allowing you to get the most from Excel. After reading the first part, you will have the knowledge needed to use the applications in the second part as a point of departure, your ultimate destination being an application tailored to your particular business.

Chapter 14 contains a quick-reference guide to Excel. If you use Excel infrequently and need a quick reminder of how to use a particular feature, check here.

Whatever your needs may be from a spreadsheet, Excel will deliver—and with thoroughness and indisputable accuracy. But Excel's crowning achievement is this: The most powerful spreadsheet program currently available is also one of the easiest to learn and one of the simplest to use! But then, would you expect any less from a program in the Macintosh tradition?

John R. Adler

DYNAMICS OF MACINTOSH EXCEL

DYNAMICS OF MACINTOSH EXCEL®

JOHN R. ADLER

250340

DOW JONES-IRWIN
Homewood, Illinois   60430

© DOW JONES-IRWIN, 1987

This publication is designed to provide accurate and authoritative information in regard to the subject matter covered. It is sold with the understanding that the publisher is not engaged in rendering legal, accounting, or other professional service. If legal advice or other expert assistance is required, the services of a competent professional person should be sought.

From a Declaration of Principles jointly adopted by a Committee of the American Bar Association and a Committee of Publishers.

ISBN 0-87094-907-1

Library of Congress Catalog Card No. 86–72565

Printed in the United States of America

2 3 4 5 6 7 8 9 0 VK 4 3 2 1 0 9 8

To my wife Candace

Contents

Value: *Purpose. Constructing the Model. Using the Future Value Worksheet.* Finding the Interest Rate: *Purpose. Constructing the Model. Using the Interest Rate Worksheet.* Amortizing a Loan: *Purpose. Constructing the Model. Using the Loan Amortization Worksheet.*

PART ONE

Features

INTRODUCTION

Excel has its own way of "thinking," a philosophy of life if you will. The challenge of any program writer is to bring the program's method of thinking as close as possible to a human's method of thinking, but without compromising the advantages a computer has over a human (e.g., number crunching, memory). Naturally, the program writer must make certain choices regarding how the user operates the program and how the program operates itself. Ideally, these choices are clearly explained to the user in the instruction manual so that he or she can fully comprehend the program and utilize it to the utmost. The problem is that the user becomes afraid of the instruction manual when it gets too thick. A compromise must be made, so many important concepts are covered only cursorily in the manual.

Since you have already had some experience with Excel, now is the perfect time for you to learn some of the finer points of Excel's philosophy of life. Part One will enable you to do so. Chapter 1 discusses entering numbers, text, and formulas into cells. Chapter 2 addresses the way the worksheet is displayed and the many ways to alter it. Chapter 3 takes a peek at Excel's highly versatile window capabilities. Chapter 4 explores Excel's unique function, macro, and array features. Chapter 5 sorts out Excel's database functions. Chapter 6 churns out the hard copies, discussing printing and enhanced printing. Finally, Chapter 7 reaches out to the world of software around Excel, discussing the sharing of data and Excel's compatibility with other spreadsheets.

CHAPTER 1

Cell Entries

The process of entering data into cells is at the very heart of using Excel. This chapter explores that process, which allows the user to structure and use a worksheet.

TEXT VERSUS NUMERIC ENTRIES

The contents of a cell can be either a constant or a formula. Here we will consider constant cell entries, leaving the subject of formulas for later. Excel will accept two kinds of constant cell entries: text and numeric. It's vitally important to understand how Excel tells the difference between the two. If you were to enter a number into cell A1, say **12345**, and then text into cell A2, say **Material Costs**, Excel would classify the first entry as a numeric entry and the second as a text entry. If you tried to combine the two cells by entering into a third cell a formula that added the first cell to the second cell (=A1+A2), an error message would appear (#VALUE!). This is because Excel will not allow text and numeric entries to be combined.

The above example is fairly clear-cut, but what if you were to enter **2630 Orange Ave.** into a cell? Would Excel consider this text or a number? One simple way to tell how Excel would classify this entry is to see how it is aligned. Excel will always align a numeric entry to the right side of the cell and a text entry to the left side (unless the formatting of the cell has been changed). If you enter **2630 Orange Ave.** into a cell, you will see that it is aligned to the left, indicating that Excel correctly recognizes it as a text entry.

Here is the rule: If an entry has any alphabet character or any punctuation that prevents it from being interpreted as a number, Excel will classify it as a text entry. However, Excel will recognize certain symbols as being part of a numeric entry—most notably the dollar sign ($100), the percent sign (21%), and the comma (100,000,000). Entering these symbols tells Excel that you wish to format this particular cell with this particular sign. Change the entry, and you will notice that Excel remembers your formatting instruction and continues to display the cell as per your original entry. Other numeric characters include **+ − E e . ( )**. The plus or minus sign can precede a number (Excel will drop the plus sign); the E or e is used in scientific notation; the period is interpreted as a decimal point; and the parentheses are common accounting symbols for a negative number (see Chart 1–1).

Excel is unique in that formulas can be used on text data as well as on numeric data. For example, if you were to enter **=A1** into cell B1, and cell A1 contained text data, that text would be reproduced in cell B1. Text strings from two cells can be combined by the use of a formula that substitutes an ampersand (&) for a plus sign (+). For example, if cell A1 contains the text string **Materials** and cell A2 contains the text string **Labor**, these could be combined by entering a formula into cell A3 that reads **=A1&A2**. Cell A3 would now contain the string **MaterialsLabor**. You would probably want to refine this formula to read **=A1&" and "&A2**, so that the combined string would read **Materials and Labor**. Notice the insertion of the string constant " and " into the formula. It is distinguished as a constant by the quotes surrounding it.

CHART 1–1

1234X67	Text
1234567	Numeric
1280 Grove St.	Text
(1467)	Numeric
23%	Numeric
123.45E6	Numeric
"12345"	Text
$123456.03	Numeric
123,456.03	Numeric

There might be a situation in which you want Excel to recognize an entry consisting solely of numbers as a text entry. For example, you might have the part number **7460** that you later want to combine with the lot number **XX11Z** to form the completed code **XX11Z7460**. The technique illustrated above would not work in this case, because Excel would think you were trying to combine text and numeric entries, a definite no-no. You would get an error message (#VALUE!). This could be fixed by entering the part number with quotation marks surrounding it: **"7460"**. The quotes would indicate to Excel that this entry is a text string. Try it, and you will see that it is aligned to the left of the cell, indicating that Excel recognizes it as text.

FORMULA OPERATORS AND ORDER OF OPERATIONS

Excel can tell whether a cell entry is a formula because all formulas begin with an equal sign (=). If the first character entered is not an equal sign, Excel assumes that the entry is a constant—either text or numeric. The purpose of a formula is to create a new value from existing ones. The existing values can be entered directly into the formula (=23+46), or they can be contained in cells that are referenced by the formula (=A1+A2). These values can be added, subtracted, multiplied, and divided by each other to obtain a new value, which is displayed in the cell containing the formula. The symbols for these and other operations are shown in Chart 1–2.

In addition, there are some conditional operands that are listed in Chart 1–3 but will be explained in detail in Chapter 2.

If more than one operand is used in a formula, Excel will solve the equation in a predictable order. It will multiply and divide be-

CHART 1–2

+	Add
–	Subtract
*	Multiply
/	Divide
^	Raise to an exponent
%	Percent (divide by 100)

CHART 1–3

<	Less than
>	Greater than
=	Equal to (used in a different context than to indicate a formula)
<>	Not equal to
<=	Less than or equal to
>=	Greater than or equal to

fore it adds and subtracts, *regardless of the order from left to right!* For example:

$$= 8 + 16/4 \qquad \text{Excel's answer: } 12$$

Excel divided 16 by 4 first, then added 8. If you want Excel to perform the addition first, put that part of the equation in parenthesis:

$$= (8 + 16)/4 \qquad \text{Excel's answer: } 6$$

Excel performs operations in parenthesis first, then multiplication and division, then addition and subtraction. If all else is equal, Excel performs the operations in order from left to right (see Chart 1–4).

RELATIVE AND ABSOLUTE REFERENCES

When a formula in a cell refers to another cell, Excel has two ways to find that other cell. Let's look at an example: Enter the number 12 into cell A1 and the number 20 into cell C1. Now enter into cell A3 the formula = A1. What you are telling Excel to do is to start at the cell where the formula is, travel up two cells, get the value from

CHART 1–4 Excel's Order of Operations

First	()
Second	%
Third	*, /
Fourth	+, −
Fifth	= <>

the cell located there, and display it in the cell where the formula is. You should see a 12 in cell A3.

So far, so good. Now let's copy the formula in cell A3 and paste it into cell C3. Make cell A3 the active cell and select "Copy" from the "Edit" menu. Now make cell C3 the active cell and select "Paste" from the "Edit" menu. You should see the number 20 in cell C3. If you expected to see the number 12, reread the last paragraph carefully to understand how Excel finds the referenced cell in the formula.

Giving a reference in the standard **A1** form is called relative referencing, because Excel finds the cell referred to by counting up or down or left or right from where the formula is. Relative referencing can be very useful when formulas need to be duplicated, as we will see in the "Applications" part of this book.

But suppose you want a cell reference in a formula to always refer to the same cell, regardless of where the formula might be moved on the worksheet. In this case you want absolute referencing. Change the formula in cell A3 to read **=$A$1**. So far no difference—the cell still displays 12. Now copy the formula from the cell and paste it into cell C3. Aha! Cell C3 now displays a 12 also. The dollar signs preceding the letter and number in the reference make it absolute. You can copy, paste, fill down or right; however you choose to reproduce the formula elsewhere on the worksheet, it will always refer to cell A1.

Let's try one more example to illustrate the principle. In cell A1 enter the number 4; in cell A2, the number 8; in cell A3, the number 12; and in cell A4, the number 16. Now in cell B1 enter the formula **=$A1**. Notice that we purposely omit one of the dollar signs used previously. This is known as a mixed reference. Select cell B1 and drag the cursor down to cell B4, highlighting the range B1 through B4, and fill down by choosing that selection from the "Edit" menu. Can you guess what will happen when the formula is filled in?

Since the **A** portion of the reference is absolute, the cell referenced will always be in column A. But since the **1** portion of the reference is relative, each row will refer to its own number in the A column. Thus you should see 4, 8, 12, 16, in B1 through B4. If you had made the formula read **$A$1**, B1 through B4 would all display the number 4, since that formula refers absolutely to cell A1. Can you guess what would happen if you filled the formula into columns C and D? Try it.

A quick way to change relative references to absolute or mixed references is to use the "Reference" command from the "Formula" menu. Choose it once, and any relative reference (A1) appearing to the right of the insertion point on the editing bar will change to an absolute reference ($A$1). Choose the command a second time, and the references will become mixed, with the dollar sign appearing before the row number only (A$1). Choose it a third time, and the references will be mixed, with the dollar sign preceding the column letter only ($A1).

Some readers might be familiar with the R1C1 method of labeling rows and columns. Using this method, column A would be called column 1, so cell A1 would be labeled R1C1, cell D3 would be labeled R3C4, and so on. Excel offers this method of labeling to assist those users who are more comfortable with this system from having used other spreadsheet programs such as Multiplan™. To activate the R1C1 system, simply choose that command on the "Options" menu.

You will find that when you reference cells in formulas using the R1C1 system, the difference between relative and absolute referencing will be quite clear. An absolute reference will look like this: **R1C4**. A relative reference will look like this: **R[-6]C[-2]**, indicating that the referenced cell is six rows up and two columns to the left. These labels might be easier to perceive at first, but they are tedious to type and when stacked together, they can be extremely confusing—that's why the designers of Excel switched to the A1 system of labeling.

WORKSHEET CALCULATIONS

When a change in the value in a cell causes the values in other cells to change, a recalculation is necessary. Different spreadsheets have different methods for accomplishing this; most will recalculate *every* cell, whether it is affected by the change or not. Since the user must wait for the recalculation to finish before entering new data, this can be very time consuming, particularly on large worksheets. Excel will recalculate only the cells that are affected by the change— a tremendous time advantage to the user.

It is possible to instruct Excel not to recalculate automatically but instead to wait for your command to recalculate. This feature can come in handy when you are working on extremely large worksheets, and many cell entries need to be changed. Using manual recalculation will prevent the wait while Excel recalculates affected cells. To use manual recalculation, select "Calculation" from the "Options" menu. When you are ready for Excel to calculate, select "Calculate Now" from the "Options" menu or press "Command = ."

"Calculate Now" can also be used to substitute values for cell references in formulas. This is accomplished by dragging over the reference(s) in the formula on the editing bar, then selecting "Calculate Now" or pressing "Command = ." For example, if cell A3 contains the value 10 and cell A6 contains the formula **= A3**, using this technique would erase the formula and convert cell A6 to the value 10. In longer formulas, the current value will be substituted only in the part highlighted. Be warned, though, that once the new values have been entered into the cell, the references are gone irretrievably. "Undo" from the "Edit" menu can be selected *only* before "Enter" has been pressed.

CIRCULAR REFERENCES

Once in a while, you might get the message "Cannot Resolve Circular References" while entering formulas. This message indicates that you referred to a cell that, either directly or indirectly, refers back to the cell with the new formula. For example, if you are entering a formula in cell A3 that reads **= A1 + A2** and in cell A1 you have the formula **= A3*1000**, Excel cannot resolve this since cell A3 looks to cell A1 for a value that in turn looks back to cell A3. This creates a circle with no resolution forthcoming.

Another kind of circular reference exists that *will* eventually produce an answer or a value. In this form of the circular reference, each recalculation or iteration brings us one step closer to the answer, until a point is reached where successive iterations change the value very minutely. Excel can perform this kind of calculation, and it allows you to select the maximum number of iterations or the minimum change in the value, stopping when the first of these limits has been reached. To use this feature, click OK when the "Cannot Resolve Circular References" message is displayed, then select "Calculation" from the "Options" menu. Here you will choose the "Manual" and "Iteration" boxes and select the limits described above. Keep in mind that Excel doesn't know whether the equation you are solving is the kind that can be solved by iteration, so you must accept its answer with a grain of salt, making sure that it's the answer you were seeking.

DEFINE NAME AND CREATE NAME

Some users find it more convenient to name cells and refer to them by name rather than by coordinates. It is then possible to have a formula that reads, for example **=GROSS−EXPENSES** in a cell that could be named **NET**. To name a cell, choose "Define Name" from the "Formula" menu. Excel may suggest a name for the cell by looking to the left or above the cell for a text entry. You can "OK" that name or type in a new one, in which case the suggested name will disappear upon the start of typing. Cell ranges can also be named by selecting entire ranges and then naming them in the manner described above. Excel will not accept spaces in these names, and it will add an underline to spaces in your text when suggesting names (GROSS_PROFITS).

Several cells or a continuous range of cells can be named in one fell swoop with the "Create Names" command. With this feature Excel will look to the left of the cell range or above it (your choice) for a list of names and will name all of the selected cells simultaneously with one command. Should you check off both "Top Row" and "Left Column" in the dialog box, Excel will name the entire range with the text that is in the upper left corner of the cell range selected.

Another feature of the "Define Name" command is the ability to substitute names for constants or formulas. For example, the name "DISCOUNT" might refer to the constant "25%." It is then possible to use the name in a formula, such as **=SALES*DISCOUNT**. Or a name might refer to a formula directly. For example, the name "NET" might refer to the formula **=$A$1*($A$4+125)**. This feature of the "Define Name" command is accomplished simply by editing the "Refers to:" box.

Once names have been defined, they need not be typed in every time a reference is called for. The names can be pasted into formulas as easily as cell references are inserted. Simply choose "Paste Name" from the "Formula" menu. A list of the names you have created will appear in a dialog box. To paste one into your formula, double-click it.

GOTO

Similarly, it is easy to find a cell that is named on a large worksheet. Scrolling is not necessary; instead, use the "Goto" command on the "Formula" menu. A list of your defined names will appear. You can double-click one or, instead, type in a cell's coordinates. The specified cell will appear on the screen as the active cell.

Sometimes you may wish to view another section of the worksheet without changing the active cell. This can come in handy when, while building a formula, you want to refer to a cell that is off the screen but you do not remember the cell's exact coordinates. In this case you may scroll to another section of the worksheet without disturbing the active cell, even though the active cell is off the screen. Click on the desired cell, and the formula will continue to be built in the active cell—even though it is not visible.

MEMORY CONSERVATION

Most of the time you need not be concerned with running out of memory. However, certain uses of Excel may prompt a need for memory conservation. For example, you may have an extremely large spreadsheet, or many documents and/or windows may be open at once. The switcher contributes to the use of memory, as do the desk accessories. Available memory can be checked by selecting "About Excel..." from the "Apple" menu, but the program will be quick to inform you when it runs out of memory—it will display an alert box. You will then be given the option of continuing without certain features, namely "Undo," "Clipboard," and "Desk Accessories." You may choose any or all of these features to eliminate, and this will bail you out temporarily.

A better solution is to get into the habit of conserving memory, which is very simple and does not cost you any features, time, or convenience. Closing windows or clearing your "desktop" of documents will go a long way toward conserving memory, but the single biggest contributor to the unnecessary use of memory is having more cells in use than are really needed. Excel figures out how many cells require memory by checking which cell in use is the lowest and farthest right on the worksheet. It then draws an imaginary rectangle from cell A1 to that bottom-right cell in use, and reserves memory for all cells in the rectangle. A cell is considered in use if it has been formatted, contains an entry, or is referred to in a formula. It is a simple matter to make sure that the last cell in use is not farther down or farther to the right than necessary. Sometimes, because of an inadvertent cell reference or a broad-sweeping format command, that last cell in use is much farther out than you realize. You can check on this by using the "Select Last Cell" command from the "Formula" menu. One final point though: clearing a cell does *not* immediately free up memory. Excel assumes that you may want to use that cell again soon. Only saving the worksheet to disk and then reopening the worksheet will free up that newly conserved memory.

ERROR MESSAGES

No matter how careful you are, you will undoubtedly receive your fair share of error messages. This is your constitutional right as a computer owner, and you should complain bitterly if you don't receive any. The designers of Excel have thoughtfully placed an exclamation point (!) at the end of their error messages so that you will feel all the more humiliated. Eventually, you will go through the frustrating experience of not being able to figure out *why* that pesky little thing won't go away. Perhaps at that dire time of need you can turn to the list in Chart 1–5 for assistance.

CHART 1–5

#VALUE!	This usually means that you have combined a text and numeric reference in the same formula.
#NAME!	Excel can't find that name you referred to in a formula. Did you misspell it? Delete it? Maybe you wanted to put a text constant in the formula but forgot to put quotes around it.
#REF!	The formula contains a reference that has been deleted or perhaps never existed.
#NUM!	You call *that* a number! We're sorry, but that just won't do in this particular formula. You're working with Excel here, Bub.
#DIV/0!	You are trying to divide a number by zero. This often pops up when a cell that previously had a value has been cleared.
#NULL!	The two sets of ranges in the formula do not intersect.
#####	This is not really an error, so you are spared the exclamation point. The number in this formatted cell is too wide for the column. Not to worry: just widen the column (or narrow the number).

CHAPTER 2

Worksheet Display

Excel provides you with many ways to alter the appearance of your worksheet. Aesthetics, readability, easy comprehension, and even accuracy are considerations in choosing how the worksheet will appear on screen and on paper.

NUMBER FORMATS

Undoubtedly, the most frequently used display feature is the formatting of numbers. Your numbers can appear as dollars, dollars and cents, percentages, exponents, with commas, with parenthesis, with a decimal point and any specified number of places on either side, and rounded off or accurate to as many as 14 places. These choices are made with the "Number..." command from the "Format" menu. When you first enter a number into an unformatted cell, the number is displayed in what is referred to as the General format. This format simply displays the number as is, with no frills and no rounding off. If the number is too long to fit in the column, the number will be displayed in scientific notation (e.g., the number **1234567890123** will be displayed in a column set at the standard width as **1.2345E+12**). A number that is too long and includes decimals will be truncated (e.g., the number **12345.6789012** will be displayed in a standard width cell as **12345.6789**). Once a cell has been formatted and no longer displays in the General format, a number that is too long appears as a series of sharps (**#########**).

Excel offers 19 "prefabricated" formats, 10 of which apply to numbers, with the remaining 9 applying to the date and time display. Ranges of cells can be formatted by selecting them and then using the "Number..." command from the "Format" menu. Alternatively, if only a few cells need to be formatted, it is often quicker to type in the format along with the number (e.g., type in a dollar sign with the number — **$123**). The cell will then be formatted the way you specified for that entry and all future entries. Be warned, though, that Excel will try to match what you have typed to one of its existing formats. Confusion can result, particularly in the specification of decimal places, so be careful. (See Chart 2–1.)

Note that the numbers used for calculations are the numbers that appear on the formula bar, not the numbers that are displayed in the cell. For example, if the number **12345.67** was rounded off to be displayed as **12346** and was multiplied by 2, the answer Excel would arrive at is **24691.34** and *not* **24692**.

This discrepancy between the displayed value and the actual value can cause confusion in certain situations. For example, if three cells were formatted to display integers and the values: **300.3**

CHART 2–1

If You Enter 12345.678 into a Cell Formatted as:	It Will Be Displayed as:	Notes
General	12345.678	
0	12346	Rounds off last place
0.00	12345.68	Rounds off to two decimal places
#,##0	12,346	Displays commas
#,##0.00	12,345.68	Displays commas and two decimal places
$#,##0;($#,##0)	$12,346	Displays negative numbers in parentheses
$#,##0.00;($#,##0.00)	$12,345.68	Displays negative numbers in parentheses
0%	1234568%	Moves decimal two places to the right
0.00%	1234567.80%	Moves decimal two places to the right and displays two decimal places
0.00E+00	1.23E+04	Exponential format

and **200.4** were entered into two cells with the sum to be displayed in a third cell, the addition would look like this:

$$300$$
$$+\ 200$$
$$=\ 501$$

The explanation is that all decimals were rounded up or down for display purposes but left intact for the calculation:

$$300.3$$
$$+\ 200.4$$
$$=\ 500.7$$

To get around this problem, Excel offers a command on the "Options" menu called "Precision As Displayed" that will perform calculations based on the numbers displayed rather than the underlying values.

You can create your own number formats if the ones supplied by Excel do not suit your needs. This can be done by editing Excel's existing formats or creating your own formats from scratch. To edit an existing format, select it and it will appear in the dialog box. Place the insertion point where you wish to edit. When you're done, press "Enter" and your new format will appear with the list of others. The original list will not be affected. Or you can create your own format from scratch by simply typing without selecting any of Excel's existing formats. What you type will appear in the dialog box. Press "Enter" when you're done, and your new format will appear with the existing ones.

Chart 2–2 is taken from the Excel instruction manual. It explains the various symbols that are used when creating formats.

When you save the file, your custom formats will be saved as well. They will be available for your use when you reopen the file. However, any new files will not contain your custom format unless you type it in anew or cut and paste cells containing that format from the old worksheet. If you create a format that you intend to use often, save a blank worksheet with that format included and open that worksheet every time you begin fresh. To preserve the template for next time, it will be necessary to use the "Save As..." command before you enter any data. This technique can be used to preserve not only custom formats but also custom column widths, alignments, fonts, and miscellaneous display settings.

CHART 2–2

Symbol	Meaning
General	Display the number in the General format.
0	Digit placeholder. If the number has fewer digits on either side of the decimal point than there are zeros on either side of the decimal point in the format, then Excel displays the extra zeros. If the number has more digits to the right of the decimal point than there are zeros to the right in the format, Excel rounds the number to as many decimal places as there are zeros to the right. If the number has more digits to the left of the decimal point than there are zeros to the left in the format, Excel displays the extra digits.
#	Digit placeholder. Follows the same rules for 0 above, except that Excel does not display extra zeros if the number has fewer digits on either side of the decimal point than there are #'s on either side in the format.
.	Decimal point. This symbol determines how many digits (0's or #'s) Excel displays to the right and left of the decimal point. If the format contains only #'s to the left of this symbol, Excel begins numbers smaller than 1 with a decimal point. To avoid this, you should use 0 as the first digit placeholder to the left of the decimal point instead of #.
%	Percentage. Excel multiplies by 100 and inserts the % character.
,	Thousands separator. Excel separates thousands by commas if the format contains a comma surrounded by #'s or 0's.
E− E+ e− e+	Scientific format. If a format contains one 0 or # to the right of an E−, E+, e−, or e+, Excel displays the number in scientific format and inserts an E or e. The number of 0's or #'s to the right determines the number of digits in the exponent. Use E− or e− to place a negative sign by negative exponents. Use E+ or e+ to place a negative sign by negative exponents and a positive sign by positive exponents.
: $ − + ( ) space	Display that character. To display a character other than one of these, use a backslash (\) or enclose the character in double quotation marks (" ").
\	Display the next character in the format. Excel does not display the backslash.
*	Repeat the next character in the format enough times to fill the column width. You cannot have more than one asterisk in one part of a format.
"Text"	Display the text inside the double quotation marks.

DATE AND TIME FORMATS

Excel's method for internally calculating dates and times can be confusing at first glance, since it converts them into serial numbers that look nothing like a date or a time. The explanation is quite simple though, and with it comes an understanding of how Excel can be so versatile in its calculation and display of dates and times.

Begin with the date January 1, 1904, and count forward in days to today. This might be a cumbersome calculation for you, but Excel can do it in an instant. (Don't worry; there are many things *you* can do that Excel can't, so don't feel insecure!) Anyway, the cryptic numbers used by Excel to represent dates are arrived at in just this manner. For example, January 2, 1904, one day after Excel's starting point, is represented by the number 1.

Excel has a built-in function that converts dates from a form humans can deal with to its serial numbers. The function is:

$$=DATE(yy,mm,dd)$$

Be careful because the order is transposed from the order you are used to. It's easy to remember, though, because it descends from the longest period (a year) to the shortest (a day). If you enter this function into a cell and fill in the date, Excel will display its serial number. Years past 1999 are entered with a three-digit number; for example, the date January 1, 2000, is entered as **=DATE (100,1,1)**.

There is an even simpler way to enter a date into a cell. Do you remember how Excel would format a cell automatically if you entered a number in a predefined Excel format? The same thing applies to dates. Hence, you can enter a date into one of Excel's four date formats and Excel will recognize it. The formats are shown in Chart 2–3.

Excel also has a number to represent time. This number is a decimal fraction that represents how much time has elapsed since

---

CHART 2–3

m/d/yy	9/22/51
d-mmm-yy	22-Sep-51
d-mmm	22-Sep
mmm-yy	Sep-51

midnight. For example, the number .5 represents 12 o'clock noon, or exactly .5 (one half) of a day. As with the date, Excel has a built-in time function:

$$=TIME(hh,mm,ss)$$

For example, to enter 8:21 A.M. into a cell, use the formula **=TIME(8,21,0)**. The seconds are optional, but the final comma must be typed whether or not they are included. Thus **=TIME (8,21,)** would be acceptable. This function uses 24-hour military time, so the P.M. hours are expressed as the numbers from 13 through 23; midnight (12 P.M.) is expressed as a zero.

Once again, the awkward formula above can be avoided, since Excel allows you to type in a time in one of its predefined formats. These are shown in Chart 2–4.

Naturally, Excel has the versatility to allow you to design your own date and time formats if none of the Excel formats suit you. This is done in the same manner and with the same alternatives as the custom number formats described earlier. Chart 2–5 contains the instruction manual's description of the symbols used to create date and time formats.

OTHER FORMAT COMMANDS

In the first chapter we mentioned a method for determining whether Excel considered an entry text or numeric—that method is to see whether the entry is aligned to the left (text) or to the right (numeric). This is the General or default alignment format. In the General format error messages are centered so that you can distinguish them from entries. If you wish to align the contents of a cell in a way other than the General format, simply select the cell and use the "Alignment" command from the "Format" menu. The choices found there are self-explanatory, except perhaps "Fill,"

CHART 2–4

h:mm AM/PM	2:35 PM
h:mm:ss AM/PM	2:35:08 PM
h:mm	14:35
h:mm:ss	·14:35:08
m/d/yy h:mm	9/22/51 14:35

CHART 2–5

---

m mm mmm mmmm	Display the month as a number without leading zeros (1–12), as a number with leading zeros (01–12), as an abbreviation (Jan–Dec), or as a full name (January–December). If you use m or mm immediately after the h or hh symbol, Excel displays the minute rather than the month.
d dd ddd dddd	Display the day as a number without leading zeros (1–31), as a number with leading zeros (01–31), as an abbreviation (Sun–Sat), or as a full name (Sunday–Saturday).
yy yyyy	Display the year as a two-digit number (00–99) or as a four-digit number (1904–2040).
h hh	Display the number as an hour without leading zeros (0–23) or as a number with leading zeros (00–23). If the format contains an AM or PM, the hour is based on the 12-hour clock. Otherwise, the hour is based on the 24-hour clock.
m mm	Display the minute as a number without leading zeros (0–59) or as a number with leading zeros (00–59). The m or mm must appear after an h or hh, or Excel displays the month rather than the minute.
s ss	Display the second as a number without leading zeros (0–59) or as a number with leading zeros (00–59).
AM/PM am/pm A/P a/p	Display the hour using a 12-hour clock. Excel displays an AM, am, A, or a in place for times up until noon and a PM, pm, P, or p for times between noon and midnight.

---

which allows you to fill up the entire width of a cell by repeating whatever is entered there. Among other uses, this command allows separation borders to be drawn with hyphens or asterisks. If you later decide to alter the width of the cell in question, the pattern displayed there will be altered automatically to fill the new width.

The "Alignment" command has some interesting effects on text that overflows into adjoining empty cells. If you choose to center text that is too long for a cell, it will still be centered, but it will overflow into both the right *and left* adjoining cells. If one or both of the adjoining cells have entries, the text will be truncated just as it is when it overflows and is left-aligned by default. If you choose to right-align the text, it will overflow only into the left adjoining cell. This feature allows for great flexibility in display. However, there may be times when you want to remove the gridlines and center some text over several cells. The only way to do this is to put the text in the far-left cell and add preceding spaces to the text until it appears to be centered. It is a good idea to do this last, since a change in cell width would necessitate a change in the spacing.

The "Style" command from the "Format" menu allows the type style to be changed from default to boldface, or italics, or both combined. To use this command, simply select the cell(s) to be changed and then execute the command.

The "Border" command from the "Format" menu draws a border around the cell(s) selected. Within the command you have several options for bordering the cells. When you go to remove a border, you might "unclick" a border only to find that it is still displayed. This occurs because, for example, the top border of one cell is the bottom border of an adjoining cell. If *both* borders were turned on, then both must be turned off for that particular border to disappear.

OPTION COMMANDS

Borders become more pronounced when the gridlines are turned off, a command under "Display" on the "Options" menu. This is a good example of the difference between "Format" commands and "Option" commands. Whereas the "Format" menu covers display alternatives that apply only to the specific cells selected, the "Option" menu commands are global—that is, they apply to the whole worksheet.

In addition to the "Gridlines" option, the "Display" command has two other options. The "Formulas" option allows you to see the actual formulas or underlying values in cells instead of the usual display, which consists of the results of the formulas or the formatting of values. When the "Formulas" option is chosen, cell widths are increased to twice their previous widths plus one character. For example, a cell that was 8 characters wide would increase to 17 characters wide. Finally, the "Row & Column Headings" option allows you to eliminate the row numbers and column letters that normally border the top and left of the screen.

The "Font" command allows you to change the font and size of the type style displayed on your worksheet. Unlike the options under the "Style" command (boldface and italics), the font command must be applied globally—you cannot have different cells display in different fonts or type sizes. When you select a font, the type sizes (in points) that are recommended with the particular font that you choose are displayed in a box on the right. You may choose one of those or enter your own type size; however, the type quality is not as good if you use a type size other than those recommended.

The final command on the "Options" menu is "Precision As Displayed," which we covered earlier in the chapter.

IF/THEN FUNCTION

Functions will be more fully discussed in Chapter 4 but we introduce the IF/THEN function here because it can be used to refine the display. Occasionally, certain formulas on the worksheet will cause a display that is awkward or confusing. For example, a formula that calculates a percentage by dividing a cell value by another cell value might produce the error message **DIV/0!** if the divisor cell referred to hasn't been filled in yet. Perhaps you would prefer that the result cell display 0 or nothing at all. By using the IF/THEN function, the error message can be avoided. IF/THEN is a "branching" function, meaning that it allows the value in a cell to depend on conditions you specify rather than simple arithmetic. If a condition is true, the formula branches out in one direction. If it's false, the formula goes in another direction. Actually, the term *branching* comes from program writing, where a conditional statement leads the program in different directions depending on the condition. In the above example, you would want to tell Excel to display one result if the divisor referred to is equal to 0 and another result if it isn't. Assuming that the divisor is in cell A1 and the dividend is in cell B1, the formula would appear like this:

$$=IF(A1=0,"",B1/A1)$$

This looks more complicated than it really is. Within the parenthesis are three elements separated by commas. The first one, **A1= 0**, is the condition being tested. We're asking whether this statement is true or false. If it's true, then the value in the cell containing this entire formula should be the second element within the parenthesis, **""**. These are two double quotation marks, a way of telling Excel to display nothing. You could just as easily put **0** in that spot if you want Excel to display a zero. If the statement **A1=0** is false, then the value will be the third element in the parenthesis, which is a miniformula in itself: **B1/A1**. You should know that what we are calling elements are usually referred to as "arguments," just in case you come across the term.

Actually, there are many conditions you can test for in the IF function. We asked whether something was equal to something else, but a complete list of operators is given in Chart 2–6.

See Chapter 4 for more information on functions.

CHART 2–6

=	Equal to
<	Less than
>	Greater than
<=	Less than or equal to
>=	Greater than or equal to
<>	Not equal to

CHAPTER 3

Windows on a Worksheet

If you think of your video display as a window showing only a portion of a large worksheet, it is easy to grasp the concept of adding to your electronic desktop other windows that display other parts of the same worksheet. This chapter will explore the many applications of multiple windows.

OPENING A NEW WINDOW

If more than one worksheet is open, activate the one on which you would like to open an additional window. Choose "New Window" from the "Window" menu, and presto, a new window overlaps the old one. This new window's name is the same as that of the original worksheet, with the addition of the suffix **:2** (the original window is given the suffix **:1**). The new window comes up sized one row shorter than the original window to allow the original window to be seen "behind" it. New windows always come up showing the cell A1 at the upper-left corner. Since the old and new windows view the same worksheet, any changes done through one window will be seen when the worksheet is viewed through other windows.

SELECTING A WINDOW

When a window is selected, it "moves to the top of the stack" and overlaps other windows and documents. There are three ways to select a window. The simplest is to position the pointer anywhere on the window you wish to work through and click. However, if that window is eclipsed by another window and is not at least partially visible on the screen, you must use one of the two other methods to select it. By pressing "Command M," you can select windows in succession; by pressing "Shift Command M," you can select them in reverse order. Finally, you can select a window by choosing its name from the "Window" menu.

Once selected, a window can be sized by positioning the pointer on its "Size Box" at the lower right and dragging. You can make the window any size and proportion you like, but notice that if a window is made too small, the scroll bars will disappear and you will not be able to move around in that window. To reposition a window, simply place the pointer on its title bar and drag it. The selected window will always overlap other windows. It is possible to reposition a window that is not currently active by pressing the Command key while dragging the window by its title bar. A common practice is to size and position windows so that two or more complete windows can be viewed on the screen simultaneously.

A very convenient Excel feature is the ability to expand a window to full-screen size temporarily and then to return it to its previous size. This is done by clicking twice on the window's title bar. The double-clicking works like a toggle: A sized window will expand, and an expanded window will contract. If you select another window while the currently selected window is expanded, it will contract temporarily and then expand again when it is reselected.

WINDOW APPLICATIONS

Excel offers several convenient methods to quickly find a particular section of a worksheet. In previous chapters we discussed using the "Name" and "Find" commands to quickly locate certain cells and cell ranges. Another method (quicker still) is to open a window on the range of cells you wish to keep on hand. This is a less temporary method, and the only one that allows you to view two or more worksheet sections simultaneously. In other words, windows provide a convenient substitute for scrolling. To move a cell, copy a cell, or reference a cell in a formula, windows can be used to immediately jump to a different section of a worksheet. Those functions can be used in their usual manner—simply select a window when you would normally scroll.

Another common use for windows is to keep an eye on a total while entering numbers in a long row or column. This is done by creating one window that views a cell containing a "SUM" formula (such as **=SUM(A1:A30** in cell **A33**) while adding numbers to the range referred to in the formula (**A1:A30**) through a second window. In this example, new cells could be inserted into the range, should the need arise, without having to change the "SUM" formula.

WINDOWPANES

Yet another example of Excel's remarkable versatility is the ability to divide a window into panes, also for the purpose of viewing two parts of a worksheet simultaneously. The division of a window can be done horizontally or vertically, or both, and the dividing line can be put on any row or column border. The division is accomplished by placing the pointer on the black bar near the end of the scroll bar and dragging the dividing line.

In what circumstance would you split a window into panes rather than create a new window? To illustrate the difference, let's expand on the example above. Imagine that we now have 12 columns of figures: **A1:A30, B1:B30, C1:C30, D1:D30**,...and so on to **L1:L30**. These columns could represent the 12 months of the year, and the rows could represent 30 different salespeople, with the figures being each salesperson's monthly sales. The totals for each month appear at the bottom of the columns in cells **A33, B33, C33, D33**,...and so on to **L33**. These cells would contain a SUM formula like the one above.

We could create a new window that views the totals in row 33. We would see about six columns (**A33:F33**) on the screen. Should we want to scroll horizontally to see the other six columns (**G33:L33**), we would have to scroll both windows separately in order to see the columns that match the totals.

But instead of creating a new window, if we divide the existing window horizontally into two panes, placing the dividing line above row 33, we would then be able to *scroll both panes simultaneously*. This synchronized scrolling is the main advantage of windowpanes. Windowpanes are often used with long rows and/or columns and totals appearing at the ends.

When would the need arise for both horizontal *and* vertical dividing lines on the same window? Let's take our example one step further. We already have monthly totals, but suppose we wanted yearly totals for each individual salesperson? These totals would logically appear in a column since the salespeople are segregated by rows. Let's put these totals in cells **N1:N30**. The formula in cell **N1** would read: **=SUM(A1:L1)**. The rest of the cells would follow suit.

Now we want to be able to scroll vertically through the 30 salespeople and see their yearly totals. At the same time, we do not want to lose the ability to scroll horizontally through the months and see the monthly totals. Excel makes it simple. We leave the horizontal dividing line in place and drag a new, vertical line to the left border of column N. Now we are able to leave column N at the right of the screen and row 33 at the bottom of the screen and to scroll in either direction.

SAVING YOUR WINDOWS

Your windows and their sizes can all be saved just by saving your worksheet. When you reopen the worksheet, all of your windows will reappear intact. To delete a window, click its "Close" box. Excel will keep the suffix numbers sequentially; in other words, if you have four windows open and you close the one with the suffix **:3**, Excel will renumber the window with the suffix **:4**, so that it becomes **:3**. No numbers are skipped.

CHAPTER 4

Functions, Macros, and Arrays

A function is a built-in formula. Its purpose is simply to save you the trouble of concocting and typing in a commonly used formula. Other functions, such as IF, which was discussed in Chapter 2, have special uses and are unlike formulas. Macros fall into two categories. A function macro allows you to make your own functions. Once you have created a function macro, you merely type in its name and leave the rest of the work to Excel. A command macro is a list of commands that you create. It's very similar to a program. When you run the macro, Excel executes the commands in order. An array allows you to perform a mathematical operation on a group of values simultaneously. It produces a group of results (an array of results).

FUNCTIONS

If you wanted to find the sum of cells A1:A8, you could enter the formula $= A1 + A2 + A3 + A4 + A5 + A6 + A7 + A8$ or you could use Excel's built-in function: $= SUM(A1:A8)$. The purpose of a function is to keep you from the tedious and often difficult job of figuring out and entering a formula. It's a shortcut. Excel's built-in functions fall into categories. The statistical functions deal with lists of numbers — you can sum them, average them, find the highest or lowest, count them, and perform other, more advanced functions whose use requires an understanding of statistics. The mathematical functions perform such operations as finding the absolute value, sign, and square root of a number; rounding off a number or converting a number into an integer; and generating a random number. The financial functions can analyze an investment by finding such things as present value, future value, interest rate, and number of periods. In addition, there are logarithmic, trigonometric, text, and logical functions. A good example of a logical function was given at the end of Chapter 2.

A function, like a formula, must always begin with an equal sign (=), which prevents it from being misinterpreted as text. Most functions take arguments, which are the parameters enclosed in parenthesis and separated by commas. An argument is usually a cell reference, but it can also be a constant, an array, a cell range reference, or another function that is "nested" inside the outer function.

MACROS

If Excel does not have a particular built-in function that you need, you can create one by making a function macro. A command macro, on the other hand, is a way to act on the worksheet by stringing together commands. You may be familiar with the term *batching* as it applies to operating system commands: a command macro batches Excel commands.

Macros can be as complex or as simple as you desire. On the complex side, macros can be hundreds of entries long. Excel's macro language contains over 125 different functions that can be used with macros. In other words, to get the full power of Excel's macros requires a commitment similar to learning a programming language.

On the other hand, most users of Excel are not interested in becoming programmers. You probably just want to use Excel for specific business applications. This lesson is aimed at the applications user, not the programmer. (For those who want to delve into the subject in greater detail, however, we can highly recommend *The Complete Book of Excel Macros,* by Louis Benjamin and Don Nicholas, published by Osborne/McGraw-Hill, in 1986.)

To create a macro, you need two sheets: a standard worksheet and a macro sheet. To open a macro sheet, drag down the "File" menu to "New," then select "Macro Sheet." Position the macro sheet so that you can switch back and forth between it and the worksheet.

A macro will act on your worksheet. However, you need a place where the macro's commands can go. That is the purpose of a macro sheet. It's like a notepad that keeps the macro's instructions.

One way to approach a command macro is to enter commands directly on the macro sheet, then run it. As you get more sophisticated, you may very well want to do this. However, Excel provides an easier way to program the macro sheet. It's called a recorder.

With the recorder you simply enter commands on the worksheet as you would if you were altering the worksheet. Your every keystroke and mouse movement is recorded and listed on the macro sheet. That sequence of commands becomes instantly available whenever you want to repeat it by running it.

In this case actually doing it is worth a thousand words in description. So let's start off.

Step 1: Activate Macro Sheet. Make the macro sheet active by selecting it. Now dedicate a range for our new macro. The easiest way to do this is to highlight a column. We'll pick column A — just click the "A" at the top of the column.

Step 2: Set Recorder. We now need to tell Excel that we are going to be using the highlighted column to enter a macro. We do this by dragging down from the "Macro" menu to "Set Recorder." When we click the mouse, nothing discernible happens. Yet, rest assured, Excel now knows that we mean the A column to be the area where the macro formulas will go.

Step 3: Pick Starting Cell. Make the worksheet active again. Pick the cell where you want to start recording macro formulas. We'll select cell A1.

Step 4: Turn on the Recorder. We just drag down "Macro" to "Start Recorder." Again, nothing discernible happens. However, as long as the recorder is on, every keystroke or mouse stroke we enter will automatically be transferred as a command from the worksheet to the macro sheet.

Step 5: Begin Programming. Now we just key or mouse in whatever we want our macro to do.

At this point, let's actually try creating a macro that we can use later on. If you haven't done so already, complete all of the steps detailed above. Now to begin, type your own name in cell A1 and hit Return. Type your address and hit Return again. Type your city, state, and zip and hit Return again. Finally, enter the current date/time function **=NOW()**. Hit "Enter." Your worksheet should look like Figure 4–1.

Let's clean up what we've written. With cell A4 (the date/time cell) still active, pull down "Format" to "Number" and take the last selection (m/d/yy h:mm). Immediately, Excel will change its code number to the current date and time.

FIGURE 4–1 Name Worksheet 1

	A
1	John Smith
2	1234 Melody Lane
3	Dallas, Tx 00011
4	29976.852337963

Now highlight the entire four cells and pull down "Format" to "Alignment." Select "Center." All of your text should be centered in the cells.

Finally, pull down "Format" to "Style" and select "Bold." All of the text should now be in boldface. Make cell A5 (the one directly below the text) active. Your worksheet should look like Figure 4–2.

Congratulations! You've completed your first macro. Now you need to complete the steps to make the macro ready to run.

Step 6: Turn Off Recorder. Remember, everything you've keyed or moused in thus far has been recorded on the macro sheet. Since you've stopped programming, it's time to stop the recorder. Just drag down from "Macro" to "Stop Recorder."

Step 7: Name the Macro. In order to run a macro, it's first necessary to name it. This is easily done. Make the macro sheet active now. The range you originally defined should look like Figure 4–3.

Before naming the macro, take a close look at it. Notice that all of the cells are formulas (they all start with an equal sign). In addition, if you look carefully you'll realize that you can actually read the macro. Can you see where you've typed in your name, address, and so forth? Excel automatically selected the macro function "FORMULA()" to put these in. It also used the macro function "SELECT()" and the menu commands "ALIGNMENT()," "FORMAT.NUMBER()," and "STYLE()."

FIGURE 4–2 Name Worksheet 2

	A	B
1	John Smith	
2	1234 Melody Lane	
3	Dallas, Tx 00011	
4	1/26/86 20:27	

FIGURE 4–3 Name Macro

	A
1	NAME
2	=FORMULA("John Smith")
3	=SELECT(,"R[1]C")
4	=FORMULA("1234 Melody Lar
5	=SELECT(,"R[1]C")
6	=FORMULA("Dallas, TX 0001
7	=SELECT(,"R[1]C")
8	=FORMULA("=NOW()")
9	=SELECT(,"RC")
10	=FORMAT.NUMBER("m/d/yy
11	=SELECT("R[-3]C:RC")
12	=ALIGNMENT(3)
13	=STYLE(TRUE,FALSE)
14	=SELECT("R[4]C")
15	=RETURN()

Naming the macro is easy. First, insert an empty cell at the top. Now make the cell you just inserted (A1) active. Type in "NAME" (you can call it whatever you like).

Now drag down "Formula" to "Define Name." You'll see that your entry, "NAME," is already suggested. But before OK'ing it, click "Command" at the bottom of the box. This tells Excel that the macro will be activated by a command from you.

You also have the option of using a special key to activate the macro. Type in "N" in the "Key" box. (We'll see how this works shortly.)

Now your macro is done. When you'd like your name to appear on a worksheet, just run this macro and what you've typed will instantly be reproduced there. Try it now.

Step 8: Run Macro. Return to the worksheet and activate cell C1 (the first words of your macro will appear in whatever cell you make active).

Now drag down from "Macro" to "Run." A box will appear listing the various macros available. Just select "NAME," and immediately Excel will create your name, your address, and the current date and time. It will then center all entries and put them in boldface. Finally, it will make the cell directly under the last entry the active one. You can save this macro and use it whenever you start up a new worksheet!

A quick way to call up this macro—instead of using the "Macro," "Run," and "NAME" commands—is to hold down the Option and

Command keys while typing "N." (For name: remember, we entered this as an option key.) The macro will immediately execute, beginning wherever you've placed the active cell. (Did you remember to use a capital *N*?)

Once you've created a macro, it can be altered to do almost anything you like. To change the macro, simply make the macro sheet active. Now edit it as you would any other worksheet.

It is possible to create macros that interact with the user. This means that instead of executing the entire macro, Excel will pause at a designated spot and ask the user to input information in a special input box.

You can use the function INPUT in your macro to accomplish this. It's important, however, to use the correct form:

INPUT(prompt,type,title)

"Prompt" stands for whatever message you want displayed. "Type" stands for the kind of return desired. Excel offers eight alternatives:

0	Returns a formula
1	Returns a number
2	Returns text
4	Logical return
8	Returns a reference
16	Returns error
64	Returns to an array

"Title" stands for the desired action.

An example would be **= INPUT("Enter 'yes' or 'no'",2, "Select").**

Another method of inputting would be to use existing dialog boxes. Many of Excel's macro functions correspond to worksheet menus. Those that do correspond have a question mark (?) after them; "DEFINE NAME?()" is an example. Using these macros with the question mark (?) interrupts the macro and calls up the dialog box.

Function macros are used as part of a formula. Instead of having a command to call them up, they are activated by the formula itself. This shouldn't be a difficult concept to grasp. We already know what functions are and what macros are. Put them together and we have macros that act like functions—function macros!

The rules for function macros are somewhat different from the rules for command macros. For one thing, you can't use the recorder to create them. Instead, they must be written directly onto a macro sheet.

Function macros are named differently from command macros. When naming a function macro, we check the function target in the "Define Name" box. The procedure goes like this:

1. Create the macro.
2. Activate the first cell.
3. Drag down from "Formula" to "Define Name" and give it a name (the name is normally already in the first cell).
4. Select "Macro Function" instead of "Macro Command" and enter.

The most important difference between command macros and function macros has to do with arguments. A function macro works just like a function. It is composed of three parts—the arguments, what to do with the arguments, and what to do with the result. Figure 4–4 is a simple function macro that illustrates this.

As usual, the first row gives the macro a name for easy identification. The next two rows are like the names of two arguments in a function. Cells A2 and A3 tell Excel what the arguments are called.

Next, we tell Excel what to do with the two arguments. In this case it's simply to divide.

Finally, we need to tell Excel what to do with the result of the division and to stop the macro. Line 5A does this.

This simple function macro will calculate commissions for us. To use it, we need a worksheet (see Figure 4–5).

We call up a function macro just as we would any other macro. On our worksheet we begin with the formula equal sign (=). Next, we indicate the function macro we want to run. We can type it in; however, since we have to type *both* the macro sheet and the macro name, it's easier to simply type an equal sign (=), then activate the

FIGURE 4–4 Function Macro

	A	B
1	COMMISSION	Names the macro
2	=ARGUMENT("SALES")	Names the first argument
3	=ARGUMENT("COMMISSION")	Names the second argument
4	=SALES/COMMISSION	Divides the first argument by the second
5	=RETURN(A4)	Stops macro/produces the result of cell A4

FIGURE 4–5 Function Worksheet

	A	B	C	D
1	Salesperson	Sales	Commission	
2	Henry	10000	=FUNCTIONMACRO!$A$1(B2,10)	1000
3	Helen	12000	=FUNCTIONMACRO!$A$1(B3,10)	1200
4	Dorothy	14000	=FUNCTIONMACRO!$A$1(B4,10)	1400
5				
6				
7	Bill	15000	=FUNCTIONMACRO!$A$1(B7,12)	1250
8	Sarah	12000	=FUNCTIONMACRO!$A$1(B8,12)	1000

macro sheet and click on the name of the macro. It will instantly be copied to the formula line.

Now all we need to do is create a parenthetical expression. The first argument is for the sales amounts. We already have that in the column under sales. For Henry, therefore, all we need to do is refer to cell B2. For the commission, we are currently calculating that each salesperson gets 1/10th of sales, so we would put in 10. (If the salesperson got 1/12th of sales, we would put in 12, and so forth.) If we wanted to use a percentage, we could use 10 percent, but we would need to use multiplication instead of division in our macro to get the correct answer.

Our formula using the macro function is complete. To run it, all we need do is type "Enter." The calculation will be made immediately.

The remaining calculations on the sheet are far easier to make. We simply highlight the formula cell C2:C5 and use "Fill Down" from the "Edit" menu to place the formula in the remaining cells. They quickly fill in and our job is done.

(*Note:* for purposes of clarity, the above illustration shows both the formulas and the results. Normally, only either the formulas or the results would be displayed.)

This was a simple example, but function macros can be quite long and complex. Any problem that can be solved by a mathematical formula can be solved by a function macro.

ARRAYS

Suppose we want to subtract the value in cell B1 from the value in cell A1. We could create a simple formula to accomplish this: **=A1-B1.**

But now suppose that we had a whole column of values in A and a whole column of values in B and that we wanted to subtract all of the values in column A from all of the values in column B and then to obtain the average of the result of all those calculations.

We could, of course, use the formula described above to fill in column C with the results of subtracting the B's from the A's. Then we could add the results and divide by the total number to get the average. But Excel's array ability provides an easier way to do it.

Into a single cell we can tell Excel to first subtract *all* of the B values from *all* of the corresponding A values and then average the results. Figure 4–6 provides an example of how this would look.

Notice that subtraction and averaging are all accomplished in a single cell with a formula that looks like this:

$$\{=AVERAGE(A1:A7-B1:B7)\}$$

FIGURE 4–6 Array 1

		File	**Edit**	**Formula**	**Format**	**Data**	**Options**	**Macro**	**Window**	
	A10		{=AVERAGE(A1:A8-B1:B8)}							

ARRAY1

	A	B	C
1	10	5	
2	20	10	
3	30	20	
4	30	20	
5	40	10	
6	40	30	
7	50	20	
8	60	40	
9			
10	=AVERAGE(A1:A8-B1:B8)	15.625	
11			
12			
13			
14			
15			
16			
17			
18			
19			
20			

Let's take a closer look at this formula. The arguments tell Excel to consider the range of cells A1:A7 and the separate range of cells B1:B7. The formula then says to subtract the B range from the A range.

Most spreadsheets would show an error if you tried to do this, because most spreadsheets have no way of individually making the subtractions A1-B1, A2-B2, A3-B3, and so on. and then acting on them all from a single formula. To put it another way, the range A1:A7 is an array, a collection of individual values. The range B1:B7 is also an array. We are asking Excel to subtract the B array from the A array.

Before we go on, let's be sure we understand that, technically speaking, we aren't dealing with ranges but with arrays. The difference is, in part, that Excel recognizes only arrays that are rectangular in shape (and ranges can be of many different shapes, even discontinuous). {A1:A7} is considered a 1 by 7 array, 1 column by 7 rows, not a range. {B1:B7} is a similar array.

Excel recognizes these kinds of arrays and deals with them appropriately. It individually subtracts the B's from the A's. Then, because we are using the AVERAGE function as part of our formula, it averages all the results and returns a single value to us. (For some functions, such as TREND, Excel can return an array.)

To indicate to Excel that we want a cell group to be defined as an array, hold the Control key down at the same time as you hit the Enter key. This tells Excel to recognize the reference as an array.

Notice the special braces {} around the formula for an array. When we key in an array, Excel acknowledges this by putting braces {} around the formula.

Let's look at the example of an array in Figure 4–7. Here we have a number of rental homes identified by street. Each home produces income and has expenses. We want to know the bottom line. After we subtract all of the expenses from all of the incomes, are we making money or losing money?

This is accomplished simply with the array formula:

$$\{=\text{SUM(B2:F2-B3:F3)}\}$$

This formula tells Excel to subtract the B3:F3 array from the B2:F2 array, then add up the results and display their sum. Unfortunately, we're losing money.

FIGURE 4–7 Array 2

	File	Edit	Formula	Format	Data	Options	Macro	Window
	B5		{=SUM(B2:F2-B3:F3)}					

ARRAY2

	A	B	C	D	E	F	
1		Rutgers St.	Hazeltine Rd.	Powers Park	Mission Rd	Jays Way	
2	Income	700	1000	575	800	950	
3	Expenses	1000	950	550	900	700	
4							
5	Profit/Loss	=SUM(B2:F2-B3:F3)	-25				
6							
7							
8							
9							
10							
11							
12							
13							
14							
15							
16							
17							
18							
19							
20							

ARRAY RULES

In general, arrays don't require special rules, but there are exceptions. Once we've designated a rectangular area as an array, we can't mess with it. We can't go into individual cells and add formulas, for example. This would prevent Excel from carrying out its array function, and Excel will tell us that we are conducting an illegal activity.

Also, when editing, we must remember to hold down the Control key after our edit. Otherwise, Excel will forget that we are dealing with an array.

Arrays are very useful tools. As with any new function, you must practice using them to become proficient with them. The time will be well spent because you will find many uses for arrays once you get to know them.

CHAPTER 5

Data Processing

A database is a mass of information that can be sorted and/or manipulated. Discrete pieces of that information can be found or extracted as the user desires. A mailing list is a good example of a database. In data processing the mailing list might be sorted so that the names in the list would be arranged alphabetically, by street name, by zip code, or in some other fashion. Extracting might be calling up a particular name or group of names from the list. Excel provides a simple data processor that can both sort a database and extract information from it.

PARTS OF A DATABASE

The database itself is the complete set of information that we want to manipulate. As noted above, it could be all the names and addresses on a mailing list. It could also be a group of phone numbers or the records of patients in a doctor's office.

The database is divided into records, which are the entries. In a mailing list, for example, **John Smith, 18 Maple Grove Lane, Los Angeles, CA 90001** would be a record. Records are divided into fields. In the mailing list the fields would be called NAME, ADDRESS, CITY, STATE, and ZIP (see Chart 5–1).

CREATING A DATABASE

The first step to data processing is the creation of the database. Excel provides an easy method for entering information. We simply

CHART 5–1

Field Names	Field Entries Constituting One Record
NAME	John Smith
ADDRESS	328 Maple
CITY	Los Angeles
STATE	California
ZIP	92316

use the columns as fields and the rows as records. Figure 5-1 is a typical mailing list example. (*Note:* The first row *must* include the names of the fields.)

Notice the headings at the top of each column. These are the field names. Also notice that each row is a separate record. Row 5, for example, is a record of Joyce Allen. You can place as many entries in the database as you like and make it as big as you like (as long as it maintains the column/row shape we've just described) up to the memory limits of your Mac and the sheet size of Excel.

Once we've completed the database, we must tell Excel this. (Otherwise, Excel won't recognize our entries as a database but will treat them like any other worksheet entries.) We do that simply by highlighting *all* the entries in the database, then dragging down from "Data" to "Set Database."

Although nothing noticeable happens, Excel has now recorded and named our range as a database range. (In fact, we can refer to it as "Database" in our other dealings on the worksheet.)

We can add, delete, copy, paste, or edit with our database as we would with any other worksheet entry. It's important to remember,

FIGURE 5–1   Database 1

	A	B	C	D
1	Name	Address	City	State
2	Woll, Lorry	50 Andrews	Chicago	IL
3	Smith, Marshall	5 Zebra	New York	NY
4	Jones, Henry	123 Maple	New York	NY
5	Allen, Joyce	1111 Main	New York	NY

however, that if we add fields (columns) or records (rows) *outside* the database range, we will then have to use "Set Database" again to redefine it for Excel. (If we use the "Insert" command from the "Edit" menu, Excel automatically extends the range.)

Our database is now complete, and we're ready to extract information and sort.

SORTING

Excel can sort by up to three key references, in either ascending or descending order, either by rows or by columns. To sort, first highlight the section of the database that you want to include in the sort. Be sure to highlight all fields, not just the one you wish to sort by — the sort keys will be selected later. If you highlight just the names, then Excel will sort the names only, leaving the addresses untouched. The result would be a mess — names for the wrong addresses. It's also important to remember *not* to highlight the label "Name," or else it will be sorted along with the actual names.

Next, we drag down from the "Data" menu to "Sort." The box shown in Figure 5–2 will appear.

Excel sorts by either rows or columns. For most database purposes you will sort by rows. (Sorting by columns can be useful if you are dealing exclusively with values.)

The first key will already have the suggested reference $A$2, indicating the top of the column to sort by. Now we must decide whether we want to sort in ascending or descending order. Ascending order is 123,A–Z; descending order is Z–A,321. Let's say we want to sort by ascending order, A–Z, so we enter that selection.

Now we're ready to sort. (*Note:* For duplications in the first key column, Excel provides a second key reference. For further duplications we have a third key.)

When we press "Enter," Excel will automatically sort by names (see Figure 5–3).

If you wish to sort by first name only or by street name (instead of street number), you must create separate columns (fields) for those data.

FINDING

Finding information in our database involves having Excel compare all or perhaps a specified group of records with criteria that

FIGURE 5–2 Data Sort Box

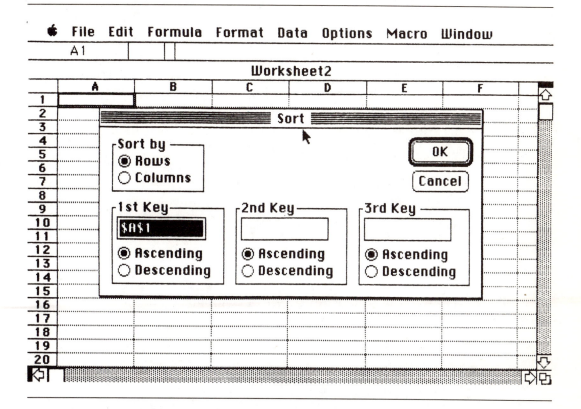

FIGURE 5–3 Database 2

	A	B	C
1	BEFORE SORT	AFTER SORT	
2	Name	Name	
3	Woll, Lorry	Allen, Joyce	
4	Smith, Marshall	Jones, Henry	
5	Jones, Henry	Smith, Marshall	
6	Allen, Joyce	Woll, Lorry	

we establish. When a particular record meets those criteria, Excel will display it for us.

Therefore, the first step to finding information is the creation of criteria. This is accomplished through the creation of a criteria range.

CREATING A CRITERIA RANGE

A criteria range has two elements. The first is the row of field names that allows Excel to identify the fields. The second is the criteria themselves. To start, pick any row outside the database and copy the field names from the database to it (row 1 in our example). The criteria range must have the same field names as the database range.

Now tell Excel what the criteria range is. Highlight the row with the names in it *as well as at least one row below it*. We tell Excel that this is the criteria range by pulling down from the "Data" menu to "Set Criteria." As with the naming of the database, Excel now calls this area "Criteria" and it can be used in formulas and elsewhere in Excel (see Figure 5–4). (*Note:* There can only be one active criteria range on a worksheet at a time.)

We highlighted the row below the field names because that is where we will put our criteria. Excel criteria can be of two kinds. The first kind is comparison criteria: Excel compares the criteria with the database and finds matchups. The second kind is calculated criteria, for which Excel does a calculation (such as locating a "lesser amount than" or a "greater amount than").

SPECIFYING CRITERIA

Suppose that we want to find all the records in our database that list Illinois as the state. Accomplishing this is quite simple. We just type "IL" (since abbreviations have been used) under "State" in the criteria range. (Remember that with Excel capitalization doesn't

FIGURE 5–4 Database 3

	A	B	C	D	E	F
1	Name	Address	City	State		
2	Woll, Lorry	50 Andrews	Chicago	IL		
3	Smith, Marshall	5 Zebra	New York	NY		
4	Jones, Henry	123 Maple	New York	NY		
5	Allen, Joyce	1111 Main	New York	NY		
6						
7						
8	Name	Address	City	State	(Criteria Range)	
9						

matter.) Now we drag down the "Data" menu to "Find." Instantly, Excel will highlight the second row, the one where Lorry Woll of Illinois is located.

On the other hand, suppose that we want to find all the records for people in New York. We would type in "NY" under "State" in the criteria range and then follow the same procedure. Excel would highlight the first New York entry, "Smith, Marshall" (see Figure 5–5). To find the next instance of a New York record, we would press "Control F." Excel would move to the next entry, "Jones, Henry," and highlight it and so forth, until all of the New York entries were highlighted. In this fashion we could search for any entry under any heading in the database and find it.

EXTRACTING

We can combine the finding abilities of Excel with cutting and pasting. We can tell Excel not only to find a record but also to place that record elsewhere on the worksheet. This is particularly useful when we want to extract records for a mailing list or other kinds of lists.

Extracting is quite simple. First, we make sure that our criteria range has been set up properly and that we have the criteria we desire in it. Again, we copy the field names from our database (row 1) to a convenient unused portion of the worksheet. (*Note:* Choose a part of the sheet that is *not* above the database, or else the copied records might overtake and overwrite the database.) Now we highlight the field names and as many rows beneath as we would like to have considered. Next, we pull down the "Data" menu to "Extract."

FIGURE 5–5 Database 4

	A	B	C	D	E
1	Name	Address	City	State	
2	Woll, Lorry	50 Andrews	Chicago	IL	
3	Smith, Marshall	5 Zebra	New York	NY	First Entry Highlighted
4	Jones, Henry	123 Maple	New York	NY	
5	Allen, Joyce	1111 Main	New York	NY	
6					
7					
8	Name	Address	City	State	
9				NY	

FIGURE 5–6 Database 6

	A	B	C	D	E
1	Name	Address	City	State	DATABASE RANGE
2	Woll, Lorry	50 Andrews	Chicago	IL	
3	Smith, Marshall	5 Zebra	New York	NY	
4	Jones, Henry	123 Maple	New York	NY	
5	Allen, Joyce	1111 Main	New York	NY	
6					
7					
8				State	CRITERIA RANGE
9				NY	
10					
11					
12					
13	State	Name			EXTRACT RANGE
14	NY	Smith, Marshall			
15	NY	Jones, Henry			
16	NY	Allen, Joyce			

Excel will then find the records we want under the criteria range and copy them to the extract range.

It is not necessary to find or to extract whole records. We can find or extract any column of information. For example, our criteria range could simply be the field "State." We just want to know the records that occur in a particular state, say New York.

Moreover, we don't need to know the addresses of the people who live in New York, only their names. Thus our extract range will have only state and names in it. Excel will oblige. It will find and then extract only the names of the people who live in New York (see Figure 5–6).

The criteria range can also be used to tidy up the database. If we want to delete material, we can put the appropriate criteria in the criteria range. Selecting "Delete" from the "Data" menu, will then delete all matching records. Be careful when using this command, as the deletions are permanent!

CHAPTER 6

Printing and Enhanced Printing

Printing with Excel is a breeze once you know the basics. In this chapter we will begin with those basics and then cover more advanced topics, such as enhanced printing. Finally, we will look at peripherals that allow you to use printers other than the Apple Imagewriter.

BASIC PRINTING

You've completed your worksheet and you want to print it out. You don't care about enhancing it—you just want to get it down on paper.

Assuming that you have an Apple Imagewriter printer properly hooked up, nothing could be simpler. Just drag down to "Print" from the "File" menu. An instruction box will appear (see Figure 6–1).

The choices are fairly obvious. The only commands that might be of some concern are "Quality" and "Page Range." "Quality" refers to the density of the print delivered by the printer. High quality means slower but more legible print, draft quality is faster but less legible. On some printers certain items, such as grids, cannot be printed in draft.

"Page Range" refers to how many pages you want printed. Excel will take a look at your worksheet and automatically divide it up according to the size of the paper you have. It will place as many columns and rows as are feasible on page 1, page 2, and so on.

FIGURE 6-1 Print Box

```
 🍎  File  Edit  Formula  Format  Data  Options  Macro  Window
     A 1           │      │
```

Epson LQ-1500	☐ Scaled Printing		OK
Quality:	○ High	● Standard	○ Draft
Page Range	● All	○ From: [ ] To: [ ]	
Copies:	[1]		Cancel
Paper Feed:	● Continuous	○ Cut Sheet	
☐ Preview			

```
10
11
12
13
14
15
16
17
18
19
20
```

With "Page Range" you tell Excel which pages to print. "All" is normally checked, although you can insert whatever pages you want.

PREVIEWING

Before printing, you can preview what the printout will look like by hitting the "Preview" box. When you are in preview, the mouse cursor will look like a magnifying glass. Just aim it at any part of the previewed paper to get a blowup of that part. Be sure to deselect "Preview" before printing.

If the sheet is the way you want it, all you need do is click OK and Excel will print out. It's just that simple.

FORMATTING THE PAGE

The format that Excel uses to print out comes preset so that you can do a basic print as described above. You can, however, adjust

FIGURE 6–2   Page Setup Box

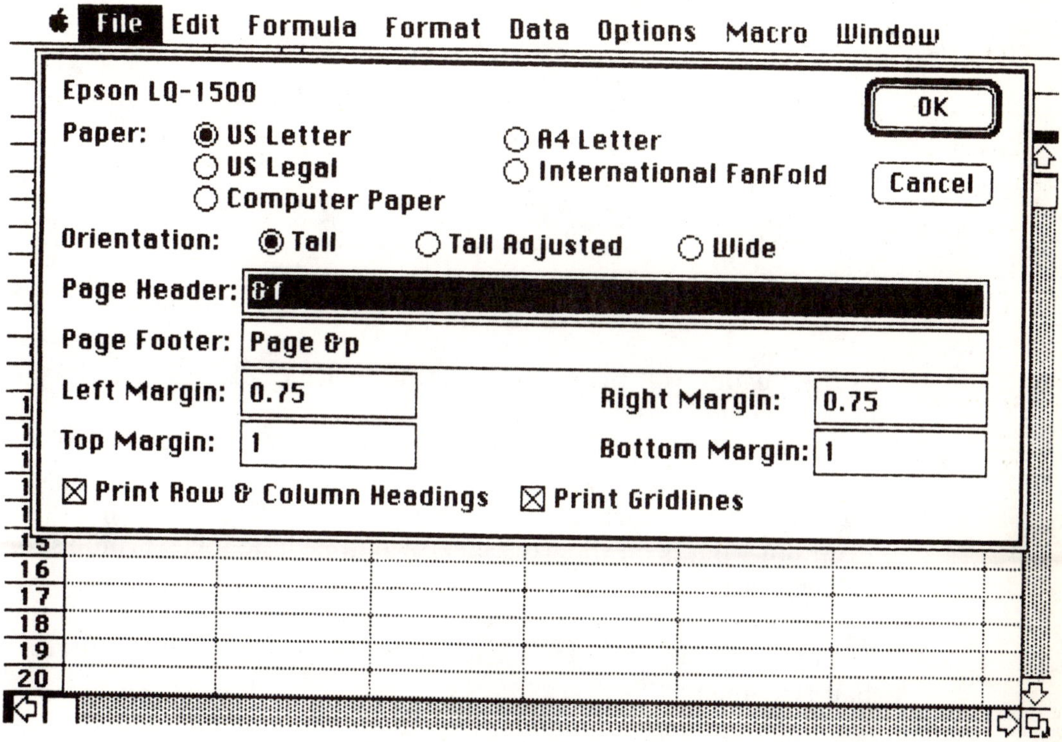

the format in a wide variety of ways. To do this, you drag down the "File" menu to "Page Setup" (see Figure 6–2).

What should be obvious is that you can adjust almost the entire format by changing the various settings here. Most of the settings are self-explanatory; however, a few comments on certain items are in order.

Excel comes with the top and bottom margins set at 1 inch and the side margins set at 3/4 inch. You may want to change these depending on the type of work you are doing.

When "No Page Breaks" is on, Excel will skip over perforations in continuous form paper. When it is off (no "X" in the box), Excel will print over the perforations.

Excel uses a code system to change alignment or to call up certain print features. The codes are shown in Chart 6–1.

The codes can be used in the "Page Header" or "Page Footer" lines right along with the text. For example, **&L&B&IFIRST TRY**

CHART 6–1

Print page number	&P
Print date	&D
Print time	&T
Print bold	&B
Print italic	&I
Print left	&L (What follows is printed to the left.)
Print right	&R (What follows is printed to the right.)
Center print	&C (What follows is centered.)
Print ampersand	&&

---

in the header will print the heading "FIRST TRY" to the left in boldface italic.

If you want to print a report (as described in Chapter 13 in the section "word processing"), click off "Print Row & Column Headings" and "Print Gridlines." With these two off, Excel will simply print out what is on the worksheet, whether it be text, formulas, or values, without the normal grids and border designations.

If you want to reduce the size of the printout, use the "Print Reduction" box. Excel will then use condensed type and produce a half-size image.

PARTIAL WORKSHEET PRINTOUTS

Excel also allows you to select only a portion of the worksheet to print instead of the entire sheet. You can select the section you want to print by first highlighting that area as a range, then dragging down from the "Options" menu to "Set Print Area." When printing out, Excel will print only this range.

Similarly, using "Print Title" from the same menu, you can highlight the titles you want and have them printed. You can add page breaks by designating a single cell and then selecting "Page Breaks," also from the "Options" menu.

These features offer great flexibility when you are printing a worksheet.

ENHANCED PRINTING

Thus far we have been proceeding on the assumption that you are printing on the Macintosh Imagewriter printer. However, other printers can be used in combination with your Macintosh and Excel.

The first option is to simply send the information in a conventional way out of the printer port to any peripherals that can accept it. This can be done by dragging down the "File" menu to "Printer Setup."

Here you are given two options—either the Macintosh (Imagewriter) or TTY. TTY is a standard interface that sends the information serially to another printer. The speed at which it is sent can be specified by the baud setting. You choose the baud rate by matching the printer's.

The problem with using this means to send information to a printer other than an Imagewriter is that the screen display is not faithfully reproduced on paper. The Mac and Excel print essentially by "dumping" what's on-screen to the printer. It's as if a picture were taken of the screen image and then sent to the printer.

When TTY is used, only the data in the worksheet are sent out. The graphics, which are an essential part of Excel, cannot be sent over TTY.

Similarly, we could send data (but no graphics) serially out to a modem by clicking the "Modem" selection in this box. Again, the baud rate specified would depend on the type of modem we were using.

BETTER PRINTING

It is possible to print out with full graphics on printers other than the Imagewriter. However, this requires additional hardware and/or software depending on the system chosen.

The first product we'll consider is the Universal Serial Interface, produced by Hanzon, 18732 142nd Avenue, NE, Woodinville, WI 98072. This product transforms the *serial* signal sent by the Mac into the *parallel* signal understood by Epson printers. (Serial means that the signal goes one bit at a time, one bit after another; parallel means that all eight bits in the signal go simultaneously—a subtle but important distinction.)

The product is a piece of hardware that installs directly inside Epson series FX, RX, or LX printers. With this product installed, the Epson printer behaves much like an Imagewriter. As of this writing, the Interface is priced at under $125 retail.

The second product we'll consider is the MacEnhancer, which is made by the same organization that makes Excel—Microsoft

Corporation, 10700 Northrup Way, Box 97200, Bellevue, WI 98009. The MacEnhancer is a truly remarkable product. It expands the Mac in ways that one wouldn't think were possible.

The MacEnhancer consists of an external piece of hardware that connects with the Mac and uses two diskettes of software. As of this writing, the latest version allows the Mac and Excel to be printed on the following standard dot matrix printers:

Epson FX-80/100, RX-80, MX-80/100
HP ThinkJet
IBM Graphics
I. Itoh Prowriter 8510
Okidata 92/93
Apple Imagewriter

In addition, the MacEnhancer allows printing on the following high-resolution, letter-quality dot matrix printers:

Toshiba P1340/1351
Epson LQ-1500

USING THE MACENHANCER

With the hardware installed, using the MacEnhancer is quite easy. It can be installed on the *copy* of the Excel program diskette or on the Excel data diskette, depending on which is used to boot up the system. Complete and easy-to-understand installation instructions come with the product. (It is possible to locate the MacEnhancer on the Mac system diskette, but this means that Excel runs using the Mac operating system diskette. For some reason this arrangement tends to produce on-screen images with Excel that are fuzzier than those produced when using the data diskette that comes with the Excel program.)

As part of the installation program, the screen shown in Figure 6–3 appears on the Mac. From this screen it is easy to see that the MacEnhancer offers three serial ports and one parallel port. This means that it is possible to run the Mac Imagewriter, a dot matrix printer such as the Epson LQ-1500, and a modem without having to change wires or fiddle around with the system.

As part of the installation, you pull down a menu titled "Printer" and make your selection. The MacEnhancer will now install that particular printer. (You can install more than one printer.)

FIGURE 6–3 MacEnhancer Installation Screen

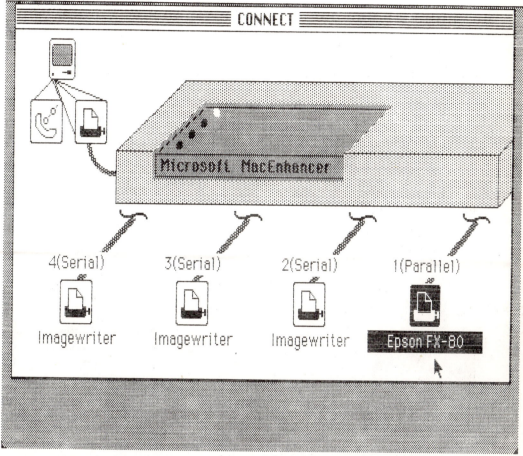

Once the simple install process has been completed, the "Apple" menu contains one or two new entries. If you installed only one printer, the menu contains an entry called "MacEnhancer." If you installed more than one printer, there is an additional entry titled "Choose Printer."

When you drag down from the "Apple" menu to "MacEnhancer," you can select the MacEnhancer port that you wish to use (port 1 is used for parallel printers). When you select "Choose Printer," you are given a choice of the various printer options that

FIGURE 6–4 Print Menu Showing Epson LQ-1500

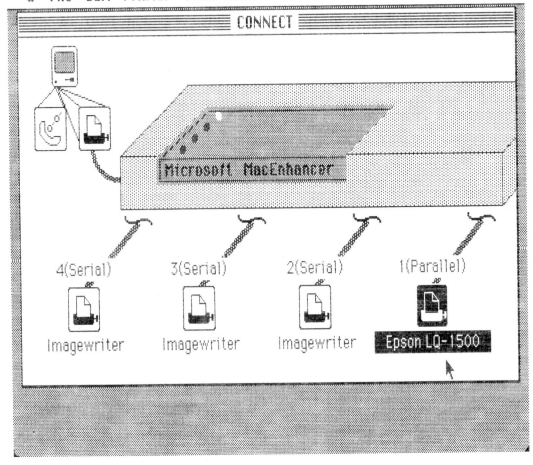

options that you have installed, such as the Toshiba P1340 or the Okidata 93. You select the printer that you want to use. (You can have multiple printers installed on this menu.)

Now the correct printer driver is ready. When you call up "Print" from the "File" menu, instead of the standard Imagewriter, the printer of your choice will appear, as shown in Figure 6–4. Printout now proceeds in the normal fashion.

The MacEnhancer increases the number of ports available on the Macintosh. It also allows you to quickly switch between modem and a wide variety of printers. Many of the available printers on the list are faster than the standard Mac Imagewriter, and some offer near-letter-quality printing. In some cases (such as with certain Epson models) the printers can be set up separately to run a variety of types and styles (e.g., two types of boldface, superscript, elite, pica, condensed, and italic) *in addition* to the styles, fonts, and character widths offered by Excel.

To put it another way, the MacEnhancer truly does enhance the Macintosh and Excel. If the printout is important to you, take a serious look at this product.

CHAPTER 7

Interfacing with Other Software

Even though Excel is currently a state-of-the-art product and could "rest on its laurels" and let other software manufacturers worry about their compatibility with Excel, the program has anticipated user needs by providing ways to share data with other software. This chapter looks at how to transfer data and graphics from Excel to other Apple software, how to convert other popular spreadsheet formats to Excel, and even (perish the thought!) how to convert Excel data to other spreadsheet formats.

DATA TRANSFER FROM EXCEL

There are two method for incorporating Excel data and graphics into a document of another program. (We are now discussing non-spreadsheet software, such as a word processor or MacPaint™ — spreadsheet compatibility will be discussed later in the chapter.)

The first method entails transferring the Excel material to the clipboard, leaving Excel, entering the other program, and transferring the material from the clipboard to the document. This is essentially an elaborate cut-and-paste process. Here are the steps in detail:

First, you must determine what type of information you would like to transfer, since the process is different depending on whether you are transferring values on the worksheet, a picture of the worksheet itself, or a chart. When values are transferred, the cell *contents* are transferred and not the worksheet. These contents look like a list on the new document, and they can be edited according to the provisions of the new software. There is no longer a relationship or connection between "cells," since Excel provides that relationship, and Excel is gone. When a cell contains a formula, the formula is *not* transferred—instead, the current value of the cell is transferred.

To transfer values from Excel to the clipboard, select the area to be transferred by dragging across it, then choose the "Copy" command from the "Edit" menu. This automatically puts the selected area on the clipboard.

The first step in transferring a picture of the worksheet is almost the same process, except that you must hold down the Shift key before pulling down the "Edit" menu. By doing this, you will see the "Copy Picture" option—simply select it instead of "Copy" to transfer a picture of the selected portion of the worksheet to the clipboard. Keep in mind, though, that a picture cannot be edited by a word processor—it must be left intact.

To copy a chart, activate it and then select "Copy Chart" from the "Edit" menu. You will be given a choice—you may copy the chart in the same size that it currently appears on the screen, or you may copy it in the size that it will be when printed. Most of the time you will want to copy it in the same size that it appears on the screen, but it is a good idea to decide what size is appropriate for the new document and then to adjust the size of the chart before copying it.

Once the appropriate data have been copied to the clipboard, you must leave Excel by selecting "Quit" from the "File" menu. Eject your Excel disk from the external drive, and replace it with the disk containing the new program. Run the new program, open a document, and copy the contents from the clipboard into the new document by choosing "Paste" from the "Edit" menu.

No other copy or cut commands can be issued between the time the material goes onto the clipboard and the time it is pasted into the new document; otherwise, the material will be lost. The clipboard is wiped clean every time a new copy or cut command is issued.

THE SWITCHER

If you try the above method, you will find that it is laborious and time consuming. The Switcher is a file designed to make the process of switching between applications as easy as a few keystrokes.

First, a few disclaimers: The Switcher is not guaranteed by Apple or Microsoft to work with all applications. Also, since it accomplishes its magic by loading two or more applications into memory simultaneously, it consumes a lot of memory; hence, large worksheets or document files are pretty much out of the question.

Now the good news. The Switcher has been tested and works well with all of Microsoft's products. In addition, the memory is more than adequate for most documents and can be redistributed to accommodate a particular situation (more on this later).

Setting up the Switcher takes a few minutes. If your need is for a onetime transfer of information, it might be easier to use the manual method described above. However, once a Switcher configuration file has been created, switching between the specified applications can be accomplished easily and repeatedly.

A common use for the Switcher is between Excel and a word processor. If you happen to own Microsoft's Word™, the chore of setting up a configuration file has already been done for you. You will find it on your Data/System disk—it is called Excel/Word. In that case, you may skip over the next section, though it might be useful for you to see how this file is created.

Creating a Configuration File

The purposes of the configuration file are to specify which applications the Switcher will switch between, how much memory each application will be allotted, and which of certain options will be used. The file you are creating now will be the one you open to activate all specified applications and the Switcher.

First, boot your Macintosh with your Excel Data/System disk. Next, double-click the Switcher file. After it has been loaded, you will see the Switcher menu and some spaces where your applications will eventually be listed. Click the first section to load the first application. This will be the application that comes up first when you operate this particular configuration file. You will be able to select from the applications available—you might need to eject and insert disks at this point until you find the appropriate application.

After you indicate your selection, you will be asked to allocate both the minimum and preferred memory sizes. The minimum memory necessary can be found in your documentation. With Excel, the minimum is 256K. The preferred memory allocated depends on how large a file you intend to create in that particular application and on what other applications you intend to add. With a 512K Macintosh, you have about 400K to play with after the Switcher and systems have been loaded. You can find the exact number by choosing "Show Info" from the "File" menu within Switcher. As an example, if an application was designed to run on a 128K Macintosh, then 128K is a good starting point for that application. In the supplied Excel/Word configuration file, Microsoft allocates 304K to Excel in order to allow for a medium-sized worksheet. This is a choice that you need to get a feeling for — once you have used the Switcher and applications together a few times, you will know better how much memory to allocate.

Once the first application has been configured, all that remains to be done is to configure the additional applications. Although the Switcher can accommodate up to four applications, with Excel there will probably be only enough memory for two applications (including Excel). Repeat the steps above to configure the additional application(s).

Certain options are available with the Switcher. A discussion of these will be postponed until you have seen the Switcher in action. You will then have a better understanding of the significance of the options.

The Switcher can be configured every time it is to be used in the above manner, or, alternatively, these parameters can be saved in a configuration file. To save, choose "Save Settings" from the "File" menu. Be sure to save the configuration file on the same disk that contains the Switcher file.

USING THE SWITCHER

To use the Switcher, you must first create two disks that contain the pertinent files. Generally speaking, the applications go on one disk and the system folder, Switcher, configuration file, and print driver files go on another disk. However, in the case of Excel and Word used together, Word goes on the disk with the system folder and the Excel program disk goes in the external drive.

After the disks have been prepared, boot with the system disk and put the application(s) disk in the external drive. Click open the system disk, then double-click the configuration file. Soon the internal drive will be ejected and the master disk of the first application will be requested. *Ignore this request,* and push the system disk back in. The reason for this is that the Switcher still has control and needs the system disk to complete its tasks. Next, you may receive a request for the second application's master disk. Again, ignore this and push the system disk back in. The Switcher will go about its work; then Excel (or whatever the first application is) will be loaded and you will again be asked for the master disk. This time, comply with the request. Similarly, the first time you access the second application through the Switcher, you will be asked for the master disk, and that is the time to feed it to the computer.

For the purpose of this example we will assume that Excel is your first application and Word is your second application. After you have inserted the master disk, then reinserted the system disk, Excel will come up as usual. There will be one subtle addition to the menu bar — in the upper right-hand corner there will be a dual arrow. Click one of the ends, and the Switcher will instantly replace Excel with Word. Once in Word, you will see the same arrow. Click it, and you will be back in Excel.

With only two applications, it really doesn't matter which end of the arrow you click. With three or four applications, however, clicking one end of the arrow will advance you forward through the applications (i.e., one-two-three-four), while clicking the other end will reverse the order (four-three-two-one).

You may also click the center of the arrow, which will provide you with the Switcher menu. Here you can change options, and eventually you will need to quit by returning to this menu (more on options and quitting in a moment).

With the Switcher in action, it is now a simple matter to transfer material from one application to another. You follow the same procedure described at the beginning of this chapter, except that you no longer have to leave the application. Just switch! There is one extremely important difference, though. When the Switcher is being used, each application has its own clipboard. Therefore, merely putting some material on Excel's clipboard and then switching to Word would not transfer the material to Word's clipboard. You must tell the Switcher to transfer the material. This is done by holding down the Option key when making the switch.

OPTIONS WITH THE SWITCHER

By returning to the Switcher window (click the center of the arrow), you may exercise certain options with regard to the Switcher operation. To find these options, choose "Options" from the Switcher menu. To select an option, click its box. When the menu first comes up, all options are deselected.

The first option is "Switcher in Rotation." Choosing this option puts the Switcher menu in the rotation with the applications, so that when you press the end of the arrow you will come across the Switcher menu while rotating through the applications. As mentioned previously, you may also bring up the Switcher menu by clicking the center of the arrow.

"Always Convert Clipboard" means that you no longer have to hold down the Option key to transfer the contents of one clipboard to another application. The advantage is obvious, but the disadvantage is that your clipboard material will be replaced with every switch.

"Switching Animation" makes the switch occur slightly slower, so that you can see one application push the other one off the screen.

"Back After Launch" makes the Switcher menu come back after launching the first and subsequent applications. This is useful when a configuration file has not been created and new applications must be launched from the Switcher.

"Same One Twice" allows you to put the same application in two partitioned sections of memory. Excel is too large to do this with, but Word could be loaded twice so that you can switch instantaneously between two documents.

"Reverse Switch Direction" allows you to push the left side of the arrow to advance through the applications and the right side to reverse through them.

"Disable Keyboard Switching" turns off the ability to duplicate the arrow clicking with keyboard strokes. When this option is not exercised, you may hit "Command]" to advance through the applications (same as right arrow), "Command [" to reverse through them (same as left arrow), and "Command \" to see the Switcher menu.

QUITTING FROM THE SWITCHER

A little extra care must be taken when shutting down for the day. Each application must be accessed and quit from individually, and then the Switcher itself must be closed. *Under no circumstances should you turn off the computer while using the switcher,* since doing so can cause files to be damaged or lost.

EXCEL AND OTHER SPREADSHEET PROGRAMS

Multiplan

If you used a spreadsheet on your Macintosh before Excel, it was probably Microsoft's Multiplan, which was the finest spreadsheet available until Excel. If you have Multiplan files that you wish to use with Excel, you're in luck, because Excel can read and convert a Multiplan file with virtually no difficulty. Everything dealing with cell entries—numbers, text, and most formulas—will convert, but display properties, such as titles, windows, and print parameters, will not. Any formulas that Excel cannot convert will be displayed. You will be given a choice of "Show All" or "Show Total." "Show All" means that every time a problem formula is encountered, Excel will display it. This choice is good if only a few problems are anticipated. "Show Total" will display only the total number of problem formulas encountered. Excel handles these problem formulas by displaying only the current cell value and not the formula. Excel can convert all Multiplan functions except for Delta and ITERCNT.

Lotus 1-2-3™

Excel can also import and export 1-2-3 files, although this is not as simple as converting Multiplan. Since 1-2-3 is meant to run on an IBM and Excel runs on an Apple, the files must first be transferred from one disk format to the other. (Watch for Excel for the IBM, coming soon.) This can be done most simply by modem, using the binary-type file attribute and the XMODEM protocol. If this is all Greek to you, investigate the exciting world of telecommunications through your dealer.

Once the 1-2-3 file is on a Macintosh disk, the rest is easy. Open the file through Excel in the conventional way. Excel will recognize the file as 1-2-3 and will convert it. As with the Multiplan conversion, you will be given a choice of "Show All" or "Show Total" for the formulas that Excel cannot convert, and a constant reflecting a cell's current value will be substituted for the "unconvertible" formula. All 1-2-3 functions can be converted by Excel, and formats will be matched by one of Excel's stock formats or, if necessary, a custom-created format.

A few potential errors in conversion do exist: Check the result of a formula containing both a negation operator (−) and an exponentiation operator ($\wedge$). Excel gives the negation operator precedence, whereas 1-2-3 gives the exponentiation operator precedence. For example, $-5\wedge2$ will equal 25 in Excel and -25 in 1-2-3. Also, if your worksheet includes any statistical functions, these can produce unintended results. Go over them carefully.

When exporting Excel to the 1-2-3 format, click WKS after you have used the "Save As..." command and chosen a name. Excel will convert the worksheet to the 1-2-3 format, but there are more problems in converting Excel to 1-2-3 than the other way around, because 1-2-3 does not support many of Excel's features. In particular, watch out for text formulas, arrays, and the concatenation, union, and intersection operators, since 1-2-3 does not support any of these.

Applications

INTRODUCTION

Applications are, of course, why you bought Excel. Part Two is designed so that it can be used independently of Part One—that is, you can immediately apply Excel to your intended purpose without having an extensive knowledge of Excel's features. Later, you may want to customize these applications. At that time you will definitely want to go back and read Part One.

You will find the following broad categories for applications in Part Two: business operations, financial statements, data processing, real estate, and investments. Chapter 13 details charting with Excel and suggests a method for using Excel as a word processor. Finally, Chapter 14 is a quick-reference guide for some of Excel's most easily forgotten commands and techniques.

CHAPTER 8

Business Operations Applications

Any business, regardless of size, will have similar operating needs. These include a checkbook, a ledger, and so forth. In this chapter you will find five operations models. They are:

Checkbook
Ledger
Cashflow
Accounts Receivable
Sales

To use any of these applications in your business operations, simply follow the instructions for creating the model, then fill in the necessary data. It is not necessary to have read the previous chapters on Excel to construct working models. Reading through the explanatory chapters, however, will undoubtedly make the model construction easier.

CHECKBOOK

Purpose

The model shown in Figure 8–1 replaces a normal checkbook. It does all of the math and keeps a running balance, with a separate balance of all entries that have cleared the bank. The accompanying macro is used at the end of a period; it closes out the current checkbook and passes all totals and outstanding items to a new checkbook worksheet.

FIGURE 8–1 Current Checkbook Worksheet

	A	B	C	D	E	F	G	H
1								
2					RUNNING BALANCE:		$1,255.01	
3					LAST BANK BALANCE:		$1,421.89	
4								
5					OPENING BALANCE:		$1,200.00	
6								
7	DATE	CK#	DESCRIPTION	I/O	AMOUNT	DEPOSIT	BALANCE	BANK BAL.
8								
9	12/2	1086	JOHN R. ADLER	1	$25.00		$1,175.00	$1,175.00
10	12/5	1087	ALLEN SCHWARTZ	1	$12.00		$1,163.00	$1,163.00
11	12/5		MILLER MAGAZINES	1		$1,875.40	$3,038.40	$3,038.40
12	12/8	1088	JACK TRAP ASSOCIATES	1	$408.52		$2,629.88	$2,629.88
13	12/11	1089	MILT SWAT PHOTOGRAPHY	1	$150.00		$2,479.88	$2,479.88
14	12/15		ROBERT JONES	1		$850.00	$3,329.88	$3,329.88
15	12/20	1090	SANTA CLAUS ASSOCIATES	1	$1,899.99		$1,429.89	$1,429.89
16	12/28	1091	BILL SMITH	0	$12.00		$1,417.89	$1,429.89
17	12/31	1092	MARY DOE	0	$10.00		$1,407.89	$1,429.89
18	12/31		BANK SERVICE CHARGE	1	$8.00		$1,399.89	$1,421.89
19	12/31	1093	RINGITIN ENTERPRISES	0	$144.88		$1,255.01	$1,421.89
20		1094					$1,255.01	$1,421.89
21		1095					$1,255.01	$1,421.89
22		1096					$1,255.01	$1,421.89
23		1097					$1,255.01	$1,421.89
24		1098					$1,255.01	$1,421.89
25		1099					$1,255.01	$1,421.89
26		1100					$1,255.01	$1,421.89
27		1101					$1,255.01	$1,421.89
28		1102					$1,255.01	$1,421.89
29		1103					$1,255.01	$1,421.89
30		1104					$1,255.01	$1,421.89
31		1105					$1,255.01	$1,421.89
32		1106					$1,255.01	$1,421.89
33		1107					$1,255.01	$1,421.89
34		1108					$1,255.01	$1,421.89
35		1109					$1,255.01	$1,421.89
36		1110					$1,255.01	$1,421.89
37		1111					$1,255.01	$1,421.89
38		1112					$1,255.01	$1,421.89
39		1113					$1,255.01	$1,421.89
40		1114					$1,255.01	$1,421.89
41		1115					$1,255.01	$1,421.89
42		1116					$1,255.01	$1,421.89
43		1117					$1,255.01	$1,421.89
44		1118					$1,255.01	$1,421.89
45		1119					$1,255.01	$1,421.89
46		1120					$1,255.01	$1,421.89
47		1121					$1,255.01	$1,421.89
48		1122					$1,255.01	$1,421.89
49		1123					$1,255.01	$1,421.89
50		1124					$1,255.01	$1,421.89
51		1125					$1,255.01	$1,421.89
52		1126					$1,255.01	$1,421.89
53		1127					$1,255.01	$1,421.89
54		1128					$1,255.01	$1,421.89
55		1129					$1,255.01	$1,421.89
56			CURRENT BALANCES				$1,255.01	$1,421.89

Constructing the Model

Open a new worksheet. Select all of column A by clicking the "A." From the "Format" menu, select "Column Width..." and enter 7.8571, then click OK. You have just adjusted the width of column A. In the same manner set the widths of the other columns as follows—B: 4; C: 21.857; D: 2.857; E: 8.4285; F: 8.4285; G: 8.4285; and H: 8.4285. With the window set at its maximum size, these settings should allow columns A through G to be displayed in their entirety on the screen.

From the "Options" menu, select "Display." Remove the "X" from the "Gridlines" box, leaving an "X" only in the "Row & Column Headings" box. Click OK. The gridlines will clear from the screen. Now we need to replace them with the ones we want. Select cells E2:F2, then from the "Format" menu select "Border..." Choose "Outline," then OK. An outlined border will appear around E2:F2. Now select E3:F3 and put a border around these cells. Do the same for selections E5:F5, G2, G3, and G5. Now select A7:H7 and check off every selection on the "Border" menu. Click OK. Now select A9:H56. An easy way to do this is to select A9 only, scroll to H56, then, while holding down the Shift key, select H56. Check off every selection on the "Border" menu and click OK. Finally, select A56:F56, select "Outline" from the "Border" menu (you will have to uncheck the other selections), and click OK. This completes the grid layout.

While you are down at row 56, select C56 and type in the text "CURRENT BALANCES:" From the "Format" menu, select "Style" and check off "Bold." Also from the "Format" menu, select "Alignment" and check off "Center." Scroll back to the top of the worksheet and enter the remaining text as it is illustrated on the "CURRENT_CHECKBOOK" worksheet. Do not use the "CHECKBOOK_FORMULAS" worksheet for layout—it is not in proportion. You will be entering 11 more strings of text in the appropriate cells:

RUNNING BALANCE:	1/0
LAST BANK BALANCE:	AMOUNT
OPENING BALANCE:	DEPOSIT
DATE CK#	BALANCE
DESCRIPTION	BANK BAL.

These can all be boldfaced simultaneously by making a multiple selection (hold down the Command key). Center the text in row 7 only.

FIGURE 8–2   Checkbook Formulas Worksheet 1

	A	B	C	D	E	F	G
1							
2					RUNNING BALANCE:		=G56
3					LAST BANK BALANCE		=H56
4							
5					OPENING BALANCE:		0
6							
7	DATE	CK#	DESCRIPTION	1/0	AMOUNT	DEPOSIT	BALANCE
8							
9		0					=G5+F9-E9
10		=B9+1					=G9+F10-E10
11		=B10+1					=G10+F11-E11
12		=B11+1					=G11+F12-E12
13		=B12+1					=G12+F13-E13
14		=B13+1					=G13+F14-E14
15		=B14+1					=G14+F15-E15
16		=B15+1					=G15+F16-E16
17		=B16+1					=G16+F17-E17
18		=B17+1					=G17+F18-E18
19		=B18+1					=G18+F19-E19
20		=B19+1					=G19+F20-E20
21		=B20+1					=G20+F21-E21
22		=B21+1					=G21+F22-E22
23		=B22+1					=G22+F23-E23
24		=B23+1					=C23+F24-E24
25		=B24+1					=G24+F25-E25
26		=B25+1					=G25+F26-E26
27		=B26+1					=G26+F27-E27
28		=B27+1					=G27+F28-E28
29		=B28+1					=G28+F29-E29
30		=B29+1					=G29+F30-E30
31		=B30+1					=G30+F31-E31
32		=B31+1					=G31+F32-E32
33		=B32+1					=G32+F33-E33
34		=B33+1					=G33+F34-E34
35		=B34+1					=G34+F35-E35
36		=B35+1					=G35+F36-E36
37		=B36+1					=G36+F37-E37
38		=B37+1					=G37+F38-E38
39		=B38+1					=G38+F39-E39
40		=B39+1					=G39+F40-E40
41		=B40+1					=G40+F41-E41
42		=B41+1					=G41+F42-E42
43		=B42+1					=G42+F43-E43
44		=B43+1					=G43+F44-E44
45		=B44+1					=G44+F45-E45
46		=B45+1					=G45+F46-E46
47		=B46+1					=G46+F47-E47
48		=B47+1					=G47+F48-E48
49		=B48+1					=G48+F49-E49
50		=B49+1					=G49+F50-E50
51		=B50+1					=G50+F51-E51
52		=B51+1					=G51+F52-E52
53		=B52+1					=G52+F53-E53
54		=B53+1					=G53+F54-E54
55		=B54+1					=G54+F55-E55
56			CURRENT BAL.				=G55+F56-E56

FIGURE 8–3 Checkbook Formulas Worksheet 2

	H
1	
2	
3	
4	
5	
6	
7	BANK BAL.
8	
9	=G5+(D9*F9)-(D9*E9)
10	=H9+(D10*F10)-(D10*E10)
11	=H10+(D11*F11)-(D11*E11)
12	=H11+(D12*F12)-(D12*E12)
13	=H12+(D13*F13)-(D13*E13)
14	=H13+(D14*F14)-(D14*E14)
15	=H14+(D15*F15)-(D15*E15)
16	=H15+(D16*F16)-(D16*E16)
17	=H16+(D17*F17)-(D17*E17)
18	=H17+(D18*F18)-(D18*E18)
19	=H18+(D19*F19)-(D19*E19)
20	=H19+(D20*F20)-(D20*E20)
21	=H20+(D21*F21)-(D21*E21)
22	=H21+(D22*F22)-(D22*E22)
23	=H22+(D23*F23)-(D23*E23)
24	=H23+(D24*F24)-(D24*E24)
25	=H24+(D25*F25)-(D25*E25)
26	=H25+(D26*F26)-(D26*E26)
27	=H26+(D27*F27)-(D27*E27)
28	=H27+(D28*F28)-(D28*E28)
29	=H28+(D29*F29)-(D29*E29)
30	=H29+(D30*F30)-(D30*E30)
31	=H30+(D31*F31)-(D31*E31)
32	=H31+(D32*F32)-(D32*E32)
33	=H32+(D33*F33)-(D33*E33)
34	=H33+(D34*F34)-(D34*E34)
35	=H34+(D35*F35)-(D35*E35)
36	=H35+(D36*F36)-(D36*E36)
37	=H36+(D37*F37)-(D37*E37)
38	=H37+(D38*F38)-(D38*E38)
39	=H38+(D39*F39)-(D39*E39)
40	=H39+(D40*F40)-(D40*E40)
41	=H40+(D41*F41)-(D41*E41)
42	=H41+(D42*F42)-(D42*E42)
43	=H42+(D43*F43)-(D43*E43)
44	=H43+(D44*F44)-(D44*E44)
45	=H44+(D45*F45)-(D45*E45)
46	=H45+(D46*F46)-(D46*E46)
47	=H46+(D47*F47)-(D47*E47)
48	=H47+(D48*F48)-(D48*E48)
49	=H48+(D49*F49)-(D49*E49)
50	=H49+(D50*F50)-(D50*E50)
51	=H50+(D51*F51)-(D51*E51)
52	=H51+(D52*F52)-(D52*E52)
53	=H52+(D53*F53)-(D53*E53)
54	=H53+(D54*F54)-(D54*E54)
55	=H54+(D55*F55)-(D55*E55)
56	=H55+(D56*F56)-(D56*E56)

Now we refer to the "CHECKBOOK_FORMULAS" worksheet to enter formulas (see Figures 8–2 and 8–3). This looks like a lot of typing, but most of the cells can be "filled" using a formula from an adjacent cell, so that only seven entries need be made. Begin with G2 and G3, and enter the formulas as illustrated. Then go to B10 and enter the formula. Now select cells B10:B55. From the "Edit" menu, select "Fill Down." The rest of the formulas are filled in down the column. Cells G9 and G10 must be typed in, as must cells H9 and H10. Then G9:H56 can be selected and filled down.

The cells that will contain dollar amounts must be formatted. They can all be done in one fell swoop by making a multiple selection using the Command key. Select G2:G3, G5, E9:H55 (you can use the Shift key for this one), and G56:H56. From the "Format" menu, select "Number." You'll probably want to choose the format at the bottom of the list, the one that shows dollars and cents.

Two final finishing touches involve names. These must be entered exactly as given for the checkbook to interact properly with the macro. Select D8:D55. Note that we are purposely beginning the selection with a cell outside the grid. From the "Formula" menu, choose "Define Name." Type in the name "OUTSTAND." Now, from the "File" menu, select "Save As" and enter the name "BLANK_CHECKBOOK."

Constructing the Checkbook Macro

Open a new worksheet, specifying that it be a macro sheet (see Figure 8–4). In cell A1 enter the text "NEWMONTH." From the "Formula" menu, choose "Define Name." "NEWMONTH" should appear in the name box. Check off "Command" in the macro box and click OK. You might want to format cell A1 as boldface for ease of readability. Now type in the remaining lines *exactly* as listed in the illustration. When you are done, save the worksheet as "CHECKMACRO."

Using the Checkbook

Begin by entering your opening balance in G5. Now, beginning with A9, enter your check or deposit information in the normal manner. If you have a number of entries, a convenient way to enter the information is to select the block of cells that you will be using (you need enter only in columns A through F). Then, when you press "Enter," the next active cell will automatically be the one you want. Notice that when you enter a check number, the next

FIGURE 8–4   Checkmacro Worksheet

	A
1	**NEWMONTH**
2	=ECHO(FALSE)
3	=SELECT("R3C7")
4	=COPY()
5	=OPEN("BLANK_CHECKBOOK")
6	=SELECT("R5C7")
7	=PASTE.SPECIAL(3,1)
8	=SELECT("R8C1")
9	=ACTIVATE("CURRENT_CHECKBOOK")
10	=FORMULA.GOTO("OUTSTAND")
11	=FORMULA.FIND("0",2,1,1)
12	=IF(A11=FALSE,GOTO(A22))
13	=SELECT("RC[-3]:RC[2]")
14	=COPY()
15	=ACTIVATE("BLANK_CHECKBOOK")
16	=SELECT("R[1]C")
17	=PASTE.SPECIAL(3,1)
18	=ACTIVATE("CURRENT_CHECKBOOK")
19	=SELECT("RC[3]")
20	=FORMULA("")
21	=GOTO(A10)
22	=SAVE.AS?("MONTH/YEAR",1)
23	=CLOSE()
24	=ECHO(TRUE)
25	=ACTIVATE("BLANK_CHECKBOOK")
26	=SELECT("R9C4:R55C4")
27	=DEFINE.NAME("outstand","=R9C4:R55C4")
28	=SAVE.AS("CURRENT_CHECKBOOK",1)
29	=SELECT("R9C4:R55C4")
30	=DEFINE.NAME("outstand","=R8C4:R55C4")
31	=RETURN()

ones are filled in in sequence. If you need to alter the sequence, simply enter the appropriate number. The sequence will start again from the number you enter.

The column marked "1/0" is to indicate whether the entry is outstanding or not. More than likely, a check will be outstanding when it is first entered, so a "0" is entered in column D to indicate that. The entry will be figured in the running balance but not in the bank balance. Replace the "0" with a "1" when the entry appears on your bank statement and is no longer outstanding. The entry will then be incorporated into the Bank Balance column.

When you are done entering, save this file as "CURRENT_ CHECKBOOK." It must be saved with this name in order to work properly with the macro. You should still have your original "BLANK_CHECKBOOK" file and your macro sheet called "CHECKMACRO" on the same diskette.

When you are ready to close out the period and begin a new checkbook worksheet, open "CURRENT_CHECKBOOK" along with "CHECKMACRO." Reconcile the checkbook with your bank statement by entering a "1" in column D next to every confirmed entry and leaving a "0" where an entry is still outstanding. Be sure to enter any bank service charges or interest. Your Last Bank Balance should agree with your bank statement.

To close out this worksheet and begin a new one, choose "Run" from the "Macro" menu. Select "CHECKMACRO!NEWMONTH" and click OK. The screen will oscillate while the macro closes out "CURRENT_CHECKBOOK" and fills in "BLANK_CHECK-BOOK." Eventually, you will receive the message "No Match," meaning that the macro can't find any more outstanding entries to transfer to the new worksheet. Click OK. Next, you will be asked for a name under which to file the old worksheet. You might want to pick a period name such as "DECEMBER" or "THIRDQUAR-TER." The old worksheet will be filed to disk, and the new worksheet will be named "CURRENT_CHECKBOOK." Your Opening Balance will be the previous worksheet's Last Bank Balance, and the outstanding entries will be transferred.

LEDGER

Purpose

The worksheet in Figures 8–5, 8–6, and 8–7 builds on the checkbook in the previous section. To each entry a number code is added that corresponds to an account number. Discrete accounts can be recorded and tracked for various categories, such as rent, supplies, and salaries. These accounts are displayed to the right of the checkbook. Each account has its own opening balance, which is carried over from the previous ledger, and its own total, which is passed on to the next ledger. After the accounts have been named and numbered, the user need only enter the appropriate code number with each entry—the spreadsheet duplicates the entry in its correct account and adds it to the totals. A macro closes out the current ledger and opens a new one, passing on outstanding items and previous closing balances.

FIGURE 8–5 Current Ledger Worksheet 1

	A	B	C	D	E	F	G	H	I
1									
2					RUNNING BALANCE:			$2,926.53	
3					LAST BANK BALANCE:			$2,496.03	
4									
5					OPENING BALANCE:			$3,357.90	
6									
7	DATE	CK#	DESCRIPTION	1/0	AMOUNT	DEPOSIT	CD	BALANCE	BANK BAL
8									
9	2/2	101	LANDLORD INC.	1	$875.00		3	$2,482.90	$2,482.90
10	2/2	102	FRED FARSOM	1	$580.70		1	$1,902.20	$1,902.20
11	2/3		JOE E. CUSTOMER	1		$2,500.00		$4,402.20	$4,402.20
12	2/3	103	BLEEDEM INSURANCE	1	$850.75		6	$3,551.45	$3,551.45
13	2/5	104	PACIFIC ELECTRIC	1	$247.90		4	$3,303.55	$3,303.55
14	2/7	105	PPA WEST	1	$250.00		8	$3,053.55	$3,053.55
15	2/7	106	LINDA TRUEBLOOD	0	$700.00		1	$2,353.55	$3,053.55
16	2/9		FAITHFUL CLIENT INC.	1		$1,257.23		$3,610.78	$4,310.78
17	2/13	107	AT&T	1	$248.88		5	$3,361.90	$4,061.90
18	2/14	108	HEARTS & FLOWERS	0	$45.50		9	$3,316.40	$4,061.90
19	2/17	109	OFFICE SUPPLY	1	$224.00		2	$3,092.40	$3,837.90
20	2/23	110	INTERNAL REVENUE	1	$1,341.87		7	$1,750.53	$2,496.03
21	2/26		JOE E. CUSTOMER	0		$1,221.00		$2,971.53	$2,496.03
22	2/29	111	LEAPYEAR FORECASTING	0	$45.00		6	$2,926.53	$2,496.03
23		112						$2,926.53	$2,496.03
24		113						$2,926.53	$2,496.03
25		114						$2,926.53	$2,496.03
26		115						$2,926.53	$2,496.03
27		116						$2,926.53	$2,496.03
28		117						$2,926.53	$2,496.03
29		118						$2,926.53	$2,496.03
30		119						$2,926.53	$2,496.03
31		120						$2,926.53	$2,496.03
32		121						$2,926.53	$2,496.03
33		122						$2,926.53	$2,496.03
34		123						$2,926.53	$2,496.03
35		124						$2,926.53	$2,496.03
36		125						$2,926.53	$2,496.03
37		126						$2,926.53	$2,496.03
38		127						$2,926.53	$2,496.03
39		128						$2,926.53	$2,496.03
40		129						$2,926.53	$2,496.03
41		130						$2,926.53	$2,496.03
42		131						$2,926.53	$2,496.03
43		132						$2,926.53	$2,496.03
44		133						$2,926.53	$2,496.03
45		134						$2,926.53	$2,496.03
46		135						$2,926.53	$2,496.03
47		136						$2,926.53	$2,496.03
48		137						$2,926.53	$2,496.03
49		138						$2,926.53	$2,496.03
50		139						$2,926.53	$2,496.03
51		140						$2,926.53	$2,496.03
52		141						$2,926.53	$2,496.03
53		142						$2,926.53	$2,496.03
54		143						$2,926.53	$2,496.03
55		144						$2,926.53	$2,496.03
56			CURRENT BALANCES:					$2,926.53	$2,496.03

FIGURE 8–6 Current Ledger Worksheet 2

	J	K	L	M	N	O	P	Q
1								
2								
3								
4								
5								
6		SALARIES	SUPPLIES	RENT	ELECTRIC	PHONE	INSURANCE	TAXES
7		1	2	3	4	5	6	7
8	OPENING:	$12,340.70	$1,565.70	$15,765.00	$3,276.98	$2,245.00	$870.00	$2,690.00
9				$875.00				
10		$580.70						
11								
12							$850.75	
13					$247.90			
14								
15		$700.00						
16								
17						$248.88		
18								
19			$224.00					
20								$1,341.87
21								
22							$45.00	
23								
24								
25								
26								
27								
28								
29								
30								
31								
32								
33								
34								
35								
36								
37								
38								
39								
40								
41								
42								
43								
44								
45								
46								
47								
48								
49								
50								
51								
52								
53								
54								
55								
56		$13,621.40	$1,789.70	$16,640.00	$3,524.88	$2,493.88	$1,765.75	$4,031.87

FIGURE 8–7 Current Ledger Worksheet 3

	R	S
1		
2		
3		
4		
5		
6	**DUES**	**MISC.**
7	**8**	**9**
8	$0.00	$321.21
9		
10		
11		
12		
13		
14	$250.00	
15		
16		
17		
18		$45.50
19		
20		
21		
22		
23		
24		
25		
26		
27		
28		
29		
30		
31		
32		
33		
34		
35		
36		
37		
38		
39		
40		
41		
42		
43		
44		
45		
46		
47		
48		
49		
50		
51		
52		
53		
54		
55		
56	$250.00	$366.71

Constructing the Model

Follow the instructions in the previous section for setting up the "BLANK_CHECKBOOK" model. The macro in that section needn't be duplicated just yet.

Now we will alter the checkbook model. Set the width of column C to 19. Select column G and insert a column. Set the width for this new column G to 2, and format the number display as General. Label this column "CD" for code, centering and boldfacing the label in cell G7. Select cells K6:S7. Place a border around the cells, checking off "Outline" and "Left." Format these cells as boldfaced and center-align them. Type the numbers 1 through 9 in cells K7 through S7. You might want to enter your own or the sample account names in cells K6:S6. Feel free to add more accounts, but don't forget to alter all references to these cell numbers with your new parameters.

In cell J8 type the word "OPENING:" and align it to the right. Select cells K8:S8 and add borders, checking off "Outline" and "Left." Select cells K8:S56 and format them as dollars and cents. Select cells K56:S56 and add borders, selecting "Outline" and "Left."

Now we will enter the two ledger formulas and fill in the rest (see Figures 8–8, 8–9, and 8–10). Select cell K9 and enter the illustrated formula. Make sure to enter it correctly—in particular, make sure that the dollar signs are in their correct positions. Select K9:S55 and from the "Edit" menu select "Fill Right." This will take a few moments. When it has been done, select "Fill Down." This will take even longer. When it has been done, select K56 and enter the illustrated formula. Select K56:S56 and fill right.

Save this file as "BLANK_LEDGER."

Constructing the Macro

If you have already typed in the checkbook macro in the previous section, you have a head start in creating the ledger macro (see Figure 8–11). Simply create a new copy of "CHECKMACRO" and edit it according to the "LEDGERMACRO" illustration. If you haven't typed in the checkbook macro, open a new file specified as a macro sheet and type in the macro as illustrated. Select cell A1, define the name as "NEWMONTH," and check off "Command" before clicking OK. (This has already been done if you are editing "CHECKMACRO.") Save this file as "LEDGERMACRO."

FIGURE 8–8 Ledger Formulas Worksheet 1

	J	K	L	M
1				
2				
3				
4				
5				
6		**SALARIES**	**SUPPLIES**	**RENT**
7		1	2	3
8	OPENING:			
9		=IF($G9=K$7,$E9,"")	=IF($G9=L$7,$E9,"")	=IF($G9=M$7,$E9,"")
10		=IF($G10=K$7,$E10,"")	=IF($G10=L$7,$E10,"")	=IF($G10=M$7,$E10,"")
11		=IF($G11=K$7,$E11,"")	=IF($G11=L$7,$E11,"")	=IF($G11=M$7,$E11,"")
12		=IF($G12=K$7,$E12,"")	=IF($G12=L$7,$E12,"")	=IF($G12=M$7,$E12,"")
13		=IF($G13=K$7,$E13,"")	=IF($G13=L$7,$E13,"")	=IF($G13=M$7,$E13,"")
14		=IF($G14=K$7,$E14,"")	=IF($G14=L$7,$E14,"")	=IF($G14=M$7,$E14,"")
15		=IF($G15=K$7,$E15,"")	=IF($G15=L$7,$E15,"")	=IF($G15=M$7,$E15,"")
16		=IF($G16=K$7,$E16,"")	=IF($G16=L$7,$E16,"")	=IF($G16=M$7,$E16,"")
17		=IF($G17=K$7,$E17,"")	=IF($G17=L$7,$E17,"")	=IF($G17=M$7,$E17,"")
18		=IF($G18=K$7,$E18,"")	=IF($G18=L$7,$E18,"")	=IF($G18=M$7,$E18,"")
19		=IF($G19=K$7,$E19,"")	=IF($G19=L$7,$E19,"")	=IF($G19=M$7,$E19,"")
20		=IF($G20=K$7,$E20,"")	=IF($G20=L$7,$E20,"")	=IF($G20=M$7,$E20,"")
21		=IF($G21=K$7,$E21,"")	=IF($G21=L$7,$E21,"")	=IF($G21=M$7,$E21,"")
22		=IF($G22=K$7,$E22,"")	=IF($G22=L$7,$E22,"")	=IF($G22=M$7,$E22,"")
23		=IF($G23=K$7,$E23,"")	=IF($G23=L$7,$E23,"")	=IF($G23=M$7,$E23,"")
24		=IF($G24=K$7,$E24,"")	=IF($G24=L$7,$E24,"")	=IF($G24=M$7,$E24,"")
25		=IF($G25=K$7,$E25,"")	=IF($G25=L$7,$E25,"")	=IF($G25=M$7,$E25,"")
26		=IF($G26=K$7,$E26,"")	=IF($G26=L$7,$E26,"")	=IF($G26=M$7,$E26,"")
27		=IF($G27=K$7,$E27,"")	=IF($G27=L$7,$E27,"")	=IF($G27=M$7,$E27,"")
28		=IF($G28=K$7,$E28,"")	=IF($G28=L$7,$E28,"")	=IF($G28=M$7,$E28,"")
29		=IF($G29=K$7,$E29,"")	=IF($G29=L$7,$E29,"")	=IF($G29=M$7,$E29,"")
30		=IF($G30=K$7,$E30,"")	=IF($G30=L$7,$E30,"")	=IF($G30=M$7,$E30,"")
31		=IF($G31=K$7,$E31,"")	=IF($G31=L$7,$E31,"")	=IF($G31=M$7,$E31,"")
32		=IF($G32=K$7,$E32,"")	=IF($G32=L$7,$E32,"")	=IF($G32=M$7,$E32,"")
33		=IF($G33=K$7,$E33,"")	=IF($G33=L$7,$E33,"")	=IF($G33=M$7,$E33,"")
34		=IF($G34=K$7,$E34,"")	=IF($G34=L$7,$E34,"")	=IF($G34=M$7,$E34,"")
35		=IF($G35=K$7,$E35,"")	=IF($G35=L$7,$E35,"")	=IF($G35=M$7,$E35,"")
36		=IF($G36=K$7,$E36,"")	=IF($G36=L$7,$E36,"")	=IF($G36=M$7,$E36,"")
37		=IF($G37=K$7,$E37,"")	=IF($G37=L$7,$E37,"")	=IF($G37=M$7,$E37,"")
38		=IF($G38=K$7,$E38,"")	=IF($G38=L$7,$E38,"")	=IF($G38=M$7,$E38,"")
39		=IF($G39=K$7,$E39,"")	=IF($G39=L$7,$E39,"")	=IF($G39=M$7,$E39,"")
40		=IF($G40=K$7,$E40,"")	=IF($G40=L$7,$E40,"")	=IF($G40=M$7,$E40,"")
41		=IF($G41=K$7,$E41,"")	=IF($G41=L$7,$E41,"")	=IF($G41=M$7,$E41,"")
42		=IF($G42=K$7,$E42,"")	=IF($G42=L$7,$E42,"")	=IF($G42=M$7,$E42,"")
43		=IF($G43=K$7,$E43,"")	=IF($G43=L$7,$E43,"")	=IF($G43=M$7,$E43,"")
44		=IF($G44=K$7,$E44,"")	=IF($G44=L$7,$E44,"")	=IF($G44=M$7,$E44,"")
45		=IF($G45=K$7,$E45,"")	=IF($G45=L$7,$E45,"")	=IF($G45=M$7,$E45,"")
46		=IF($G46=K$7,$E46,"")	=IF($G46=L$7,$E46,"")	=IF($G46=M$7,$E46,"")
47		=IF($G47=K$7,$E47,"")	=IF($G47=L$7,$E47,"")	=IF($G47=M$7,$E47,"")
48		=IF($G48=K$7,$E48,"")	=IF($G48=L$7,$E48,"")	=IF($G48=M$7,$E48,"")
49		=IF($G49=K$7,$E49,"")	=IF($G49=L$7,$E49,"")	=IF($G49=M$7,$E49,"")
50		=IF($G50=K$7,$E50,"")	=IF($G50=L$7,$E50,"")	=IF($G50=M$7,$E50,"")
51		=IF($G51=K$7,$E51,"")	=IF($G51=L$7,$E51,"")	=IF($G51=M$7,$E51,"")
52		=IF($G52=K$7,$E52,"")	=IF($G52=L$7,$E52,"")	=IF($G52=M$7,$E52,"")
53		=IF($G53=K$7,$E53,"")	=IF($G53=L$7,$E53,"")	=IF($G53=M$7,$E53,"")
54		=IF($G54=K$7,$E54,"")	=IF($G54=L$7,$E54,"")	=IF($G54=M$7,$E54,"")
55		=IF($G55=K$7,$E55,"")	=IF($G55=L$7,$E55,"")	=IF($G55=M$7,$E55,"")
56		=SUM(K8:K55)	=SUM(L8:L55)	=SUM(M8:M55)

FIGURE 8–9 Ledger Formulas Worksheet 2

	N	O	P	Q
1				
2				
3				
4				
5				
6	ELECTRIC	PHONE	INSURANCE	TAXES
7	4	5	6	7
8				
9	=IF($G9=N$7,$E9,"")	=IF($G9=O$7,$E9,"")	=IF($G9=P$7,$E9,"")	=IF($G9=Q$7,$E9,"")
10	=IF($G10=N$7,$E10,"")	=IF($G10=O$7,$E10,"")	=IF($G10=P$7,$E10,"")	=IF($G10=Q$7,$E10,"")
11	=IF($G11=N$7,$E11,"")	=IF($G11=O$7,$E11,"")	=IF($G11=P$7,$E11,"")	=IF($G11=Q$7,$E11,"")
12	=IF($G12=N$7,$E12,"")	=IF($G12=O$7,$E12,"")	=IF($G12=P$7,$E12,"")	=IF($G12=Q$7,$E12,"")
13	=IF($G13=N$7,$E13,"")	=IF($G13=O$7,$E13,"")	=IF($G13=P$7,$E13,"")	=IF($G13=Q$7,$E13,"")
14	=IF($G14=N$7,$E14,"")	=IF($G14=O$7,$E14,"")	=IF($G14=P$7,$E14,"")	=IF($G14=Q$7,$E14,"")
15	=IF($G15=N$7,$E15,"")	=IF($G15=O$7,$E15,"")	=IF($G15=P$7,$E15,"")	=IF($G15=Q$7,$E15,"")
16	=IF($G16=N$7,$E16,"")	=IF($G16=O$7,$E16,"")	=IF($G16=P$7,$E16,"")	=IF($G16=Q$7,$E16,"")
17	=IF($G17=N$7,$E17,"")	=IF($G17=O$7,$E17,"")	=IF($G17=P$7,$E17,"")	=IF($G17=Q$7,$E17,"")
18	=IF($G18=N$7,$E18,"")	=IF($G18=O$7,$E18,"")	=IF($G18=P$7,$E18,"")	=IF($G18=Q$7,$E18,"")
19	=IF($G19=N$7,$E19,"")	=IF($G19=O$7,$E19,"")	=IF($G19=P$7,$E19,"")	=IF($G19=Q$7,$E19,"")
20	=IF($G20=N$7,$E20,"")	=IF($G20=O$7,$E20,"")	=IF($G20=P$7,$E20,"")	=IF($G20=Q$7,$E20,"")
21	=IF($G21=N$7,$E21,"")	=IF($G21=O$7,$E21,"")	=IF($G21=P$7,$E21,"")	=IF($G21=Q$7,$E21,"")
22	=IF($G22=N$7,$E22,"")	=IF($G22=O$7,$E22,"")	=IF($G22=P$7,$E22,"")	=IF($G22=Q$7,$E22,"")
23	=IF($G23=N$7,$E23,"")	=IF($G23=O$7,$E23,"")	=IF($G23=P$7,$E23,"")	=IF($G23=Q$7,$E23,"")
24	=IF($G24=N$7,$E24,"")	=IF($G24=O$7,$E24,"")	=IF($G24=P$7,$E24,"")	=IF($G24=Q$7,$E24,"")
25	=IF($G25=N$7,$E25,"")	=IF($G25=O$7,$E25,"")	=IF($G25=P$7,$E25,"")	=IF($G25=Q$7,$E25,"")
26	=IF($G26=N$7,$E26,"")	=IF($G26=O$7,$E26,"")	=IF($G26=P$7,$E26,"")	=IF($G26=Q$7,$E26,"")
27	=IF($G27=N$7,$E27,"")	=IF($G27=O$7,$E27,"")	=IF($G27=P$7,$E27,"")	=IF($G27=Q$7,$E27,"")
28	=IF($G28=N$7,$E28,"")	=IF($G28=O$7,$E28,"")	=IF($G28=P$7,$E28,"")	=IF($G28=Q$7,$E28,"")
29	=IF($G29=N$7,$E29,"")	=IF($G29=O$7,$E29,"")	=IF($G29=P$7,$E29,"")	=IF($G29=Q$7,$E29,"")
30	=IF($G30=N$7,$E30,"")	=IF($G30=O$7,$E30,"")	=IF($G30=P$7,$E30,"")	=IF($G30=Q$7,$E30,"")
31	=IF($G31=N$7,$E31,"")	=IF($G31=O$7,$E31,"")	=IF($G31=P$7,$E31,"")	=IF($G31=Q$7,$E31,"")
32	=IF($G32=N$7,$E32,"")	=IF($G32=O$7,$E32,"")	=IF($G32=P$7,$E32,"")	=IF($G32=Q$7,$E32,"")
33	=IF($G33=N$7,$E33,"")	=IF($G33=O$7,$E33,"")	=IF($G33=P$7,$E33,"")	=IF($G33=Q$7,$E33,"")
34	=IF($G34=N$7,$E34,"")	=IF($G34=O$7,$E34,"")	=IF($G34=P$7,$E34,"")	=IF($G34=Q$7,$E34,"")
35	=IF($G35=N$7,$E35,"")	=IF($G35=O$7,$E35,"")	=IF($G35=P$7,$E35,"")	=IF($G35=Q$7,$E35,"")
36	=IF($G36=N$7,$E36,"")	=IF($G36=O$7,$E36,"")	=IF($G36=P$7,$E36,"")	=IF($G36=Q$7,$E36,"")
37	=IF($G37=N$7,$E37,"")	=IF($G37=O$7,$E37,"")	=IF($G37=P$7,$E37,"")	=IF($G37=Q$7,$E37,"")
38	=IF($G38=N$7,$E38,"")	=IF($G38=O$7,$E38,"")	=IF($G38=P$7,$E38,"")	=IF($G38=Q$7,$E38,"")
39	=IF($G39=N$7,$E39,"")	=IF($G39=O$7,$E39,"")	=IF($G39=P$7,$E39,"")	=IF($G39=Q$7,$E39,"")
40	=IF($G40=N$7,$E40,"")	=IF($G40=O$7,$E40,"")	=IF($G40=P$7,$E40,"")	=IF($G40=Q$7,$E40,"")
41	=IF($G41=N$7,$E41,"")	=IF($G41=O$7,$E41,"")	=IF($G41=P$7,$E41,"")	=IF($G41=Q$7,$E41,"")
42	=IF($G42=N$7,$E42,"")	=IF($G42=O$7,$E42,"")	=IF($G42=P$7,$E42,"")	=IF($G42=Q$7,$E42,"")
43	=IF($G43=N$7,$E43,"")	=IF($G43=O$7,$E43,"")	=IF($G43=P$7,$E43,"")	=IF($G43=Q$7,$E43,"")
44	=IF($G44=N$7,$E44,"")	=IF($G44=O$7,$E44,"")	=IF($G44=P$7,$E44,"")	=IF($G44=Q$7,$E44,"")
45	=IF($G45=N$7,$E45,"")	=IF($G45=O$7,$E45,"")	=IF($G45=P$7,$E45,"")	=IF($G45=Q$7,$E45,"")
46	=IF($G46=N$7,$E46,"")	=IF($G46=O$7,$E46,"")	=IF($G46=P$7,$E46,"")	=IF($G46=Q$7,$E46,"")
47	=IF($G47=N$7,$E47,"")	=IF($G47=O$7,$E47,"")	=IF($G47=P$7,$E47,"")	=IF($G47=Q$7,$E47,"")
48	=IF($G48=N$7,$E48,"")	=IF($G48=O$7,$E48,"")	=IF($G48=P$7,$E48,"")	=IF($G48=Q$7,$E48,"")
49	=IF($G49=N$7,$E49,"")	=IF($G49=O$7,$E49,"")	=IF($G49=P$7,$E49,"")	=IF($G49=Q$7,$E49,"")
50	=IF($G50=N$7,$E50,"")	=IF($G50=O$7,$E50,"")	=IF($G50=P$7,$E50,"")	=IF($G50=Q$7,$E50,"")
51	=IF($G51=N$7,$E51,"")	=IF($G51=O$7,$E51,"")	=IF($G51=P$7,$E51,"")	=IF($G51=Q$7,$E51,"")
52	=IF($G52=N$7,$E52,"")	=IF($G52=O$7,$E52,"")	=IF($G52=P$7,$E52,"")	=IF($G52=Q$7,$E52,"")
53	=IF($G53=N$7,$E53,"")	=IF($G53=O$7,$E53,"")	=IF($G53=P$7,$E53,"")	=IF($G53=Q$7,$E53,"")
54	=IF($G54=N$7,$E54,"")	=IF($G54=O$7,$E54,"")	=IF($G54=P$7,$E54,"")	=IF($G54=Q$7,$E54,"")
55	=IF($G55=N$7,$E55,"")	=IF($G55=O$7,$E55,"")	=IF($G55=P$7,$E55,"")	=IF($G55=Q$7,$E55,"")
56	=SUM(N8:N55)	=SUM(O8:O55)	=SUM(P8:P55)	=SUM(Q8:Q55)

FIGURE 8–10 Ledger Formulas Worksheet 3

	R	S
1		
2		
3		
4		
5		
6	DUES	MISC.
7	8	9
8		
9	=IF($G9=R$7,$E9,"")	=IF($G9=S$7,$E9,"")
10	=IF($G10=R$7,$E10,"")	=IF($G10=S$7,$E10,"")
11	=IF($G11=R$7,$E11,"")	=IF($G11=S$7,$E11,"")
12	=IF($G12=R$7,$E12,"")	=IF($G12=S$7,$E12,"")
13	=IF($G13=R$7,$E13,"")	=IF($G13=S$7,$E13,"")
14	=IF($G14=R$7,$E14,"")	=IF($G14=S$7,$E14,"")
15	=IF($G15=R$7,$E15,"")	=IF($G15=S$7,$E15,"")
16	=IF($G16=R$7,$E16,"")	=IF($G16=S$7,$E16,"")
17	=IF($G17=R$7,$E17,"")	=IF($G17=S$7,$E17,"")
18	=IF($G18=R$7,$E18,"")	=IF($G18=S$7,$E18,"")
19	=IF($G19=R$7,$E19,"")	=IF($G19=S$7,$E19,"")
20	=IF($G20=R$7,$E20,"")	=IF($G20=S$7,$E20,"")
21	=IF($G21=R$7,$E21,"")	=IF($G21=S$7,$E21,"")
22	=IF($G22=R$7,$E22,"")	=IF($G22=S$7,$E22,"")
23	=IF($G23=R$7,$E23,"")	=IF($G23=S$7,$E23,"")
24	=IF($G24=R$7,$E24,"")	=IF($G24=S$7,$E24,"")
25	=IF($G25=R$7,$E25,"")	=IF($G25=S$7,$E25,"")
26	=IF($G26=R$7,$E26,"")	=IF($G26=S$7,$E26,"")
27	=IF($G27=R$7,$E27,"")	=IF($G27=S$7,$E27,"")
28	=IF($G28=R$7,$E28,"")	=IF($G28=S$7,$E28,"")
29	=IF($G29=R$7,$E29,"")	=IF($G29=S$7,$E29,"")
30	=IF($G30=R$7,$E30,"")	=IF($G30=S$7,$E30,"")
31	=IF($G31=R$7,$E31,"")	=IF($G31=S$7,$E31,"")
32	=IF($G32=R$7,$E32,"")	=IF($G32=S$7,$E32,"")
33	=IF($G33=R$7,$E33,"")	=IF($G33=S$7,$E33,"")
34	=IF($G34=R$7,$E34,"")	=IF($G34=S$7,$E34,"")
35	=IF($G35=R$7,$E35,"")	=IF($G35=S$7,$E35,"")
36	=IF($G36=R$7,$E36,"")	=IF($G36=S$7,$E36,"")
37	=IF($G37=R$7,$E37,"")	=IF($G37=S$7,$E37,"")
38	=IF($G38=R$7,$E38,"")	=IF($G38=S$7,$E38,"")
39	=IF($G39=R$7,$E39,"")	=IF($G39=S$7,$E39,"")
40	=IF($G40=R$7,$E40,"")	=IF($G40=S$7,$E40,"")
41	=IF($G41=R$7,$E41,"")	=IF($G41=S$7,$E41,"")
42	=IF($G42=R$7,$E42,"")	=IF($G42=S$7,$E42,"")
43	=IF($G43=R$7,$E43,"")	=IF($G43=S$7,$E43,"")
44	=IF($G44=R$7,$E44,"")	=IF($G44=S$7,$E44,"")
45	=IF($G45=R$7,$E45,"")	=IF($G45=S$7,$E45,"")
46	=IF($G46=R$7,$E46,"")	=IF($G46=S$7,$E46,"")
47	=IF($G47=R$7,$E47,"")	=IF($G47=S$7,$E47,"")
48	=IF($G48=R$7,$E48,"")	=IF($G48=S$7,$E48,"")
49	=IF($G49=R$7,$E49,"")	=IF($G49=S$7,$E49,"")
50	=IF($G50=R$7,$E50,"")	=IF($G50=S$7,$E50,"")
51	=IF($G51=R$7,$E51,"")	=IF($G51=S$7,$E51,"")
52	=IF($G52=R$7,$E52,"")	=IF($G52=S$7,$E52,"")
53	=IF($G53=R$7,$E53,"")	=IF($G53=S$7,$E53,"")
54	=IF($G54=R$7,$E54,"")	=IF($G54=S$7,$E54,"")
55	=IF($G55=R$7,$E55,"")	=IF($G55=S$7,$E55,"")
56	=SUM(R8:R55)	=SUM(S8:S55)

FIGURE 8–11 Ledgermacro Worksheet

	A
1	NEWMONTH
2	=ECHO(FALSE)
3	=SELECT("R3C8")
4	=COPY()
5	=OPEN("BLANK_LEDGER")
6	=SELECT("R5C8")
7	=PASTE.SPECIAL(3,1)
8	=ACTIVATE("CURRENT_LEDGER")
9	=SELECT("R56C11:R56C19")
10	=COPY()
11	=ACTIVATE("BLANK_LEDGER")
12	=SELECT("R8C11:R8C19")
13	=PASTE.SPECIAL(3,1)
14	=SELECT("R8C1")
15	=ACTIVATE("CURRENT_LEDGER")
16	=FORMULA.GOTO("OUTSTAND")
17	=FORMULA.FIND("0",2,1,1)
18	=IF(A17=FALSE,GOTO(A31))
19	=SELECT("RC[-3]:RC[3]")
20	=COPY()
21	=ACTIVATE("BLANK_LEDGER")
22	=SELECT("R[1]C")
23	=PASTE.SPECIAL(3,1)
24	=SELECT("RC[6]")
25	=FORMULA("=""*""")
26	=SELECT("RC[-6]")
27	=ACTIVATE("CURRENT_LEDGER")
28	=SELECT("RC[3]")
29	=FORMULA("")
30	=GOTO(A16)
31	=SAVE.AS?("MONTH/YEAR",1)
32	=CLOSE()
33	=ECHO(TRUE)
34	=ACTIVATE("BLANK_LEDGER")
35	=SELECT("R9C4:R55C4")
36	=DEFINE.NAME("outstand","=R8C4:R55C4")
37	=SAVE.AS("CURRENT_LEDGER",1)
38	=RETURN()

Using the Ledger

Read the instructions for using the checkbook in the previous section. The ledger operates the same way, with the addition of the accounts feature. Open the file "BLANK_LEDGER" and fill in cells K6:S6 with your account names. Make a note of which names correspond to which numbers. Also, fill in cells K8:S8 with opening account balances.

When making check entries, fill in the code column (CD) with the number of the appropriate account. You can leave this column blank if you are entering a deposit or if you do not want an entry assigned to an account. When a code number is entered, the amount will automatically be entered in its account column and the account total updated. Upon finishing the entries, save this file as "CURRENT_LEDGER." You should still have the file "BLANK_LEDGER" on the same disk.

When you are ready to close out the current ledger and begin a new one, open the file "LEDGERMACRO" along with "CURRENT_LEDGER." Run "NEWMONTH" by selecting "Run" from the "Macro" menu. The screen will oscillate between "CURRENT_LEDGER" and "BLANK_LEDGER" as the macro fills in all the running totals and outstanding entries (see the "Checkbook" section for a complete explanation). Eventually, you will see the message "No Match," which means that no more outstanding items can be found. Click OK. You will now be asked under what name you wish to file the old ledger. A period name is recommended, such as "FEBRUARY" or "FIRSTQUARTER." The old ledger will be saved, and the new ledger will be renamed "CURRENT_LEDGER" and displayed. You will notice that the outstanding entries are given an asterisk (*) in the code column, indicating that these amounts are already in the opening account balances and should not be entered into the account columns again.

Always use the name "CURRENT_LEDGER" for the ledger in use, and always keep the files "BLANK_LEDGER" and "LEDGERMACRO" on the same data disk as "CURRENT_LEDGER" so that the macro will operate properly.

TRACKING CASHFLOW

Purpose

Projecting cashflow is one of the most difficult and important aspects of running a business. Getting caught with not enough cash on hand can wipe out an otherwise thriving business. On the other hand, not getting the most out of excess cash can thwart the growth of a business.

The model shown in Figures 8–12, 8–13, and 8–14 aids in projecting cashflow over a three-month period. It can be expanded to cover a longer time period. The worksheet contains two sections. In the first section, the user enters expected total sales from three separate profit centers over three months. The expected collection time is then entered in the form of the percentage of the month's sales that will be received within 30 days and the percentage that will be received within 60 days. The 90-day percentage figure is automatically calculated and filled in by finding the remainder. (These percentages can be arrived at by use of the "RECEIVABLES" worksheet.) Then cash receipts for each separate month are calculated, along with receivables as of that month.

In the second section of the worksheet, the three-month period is laid out so that known receipts and disbursements can be entered and the running balance monitored. The worksheet takes the cash receipts from the first section and incorporates them into the schedule. In the illustrated example, the cash receipts for a month are divided in half, the first half being entered on the 1st of the month and the second half on the 15th. Of course, this schedule can be altered to conform with your business.

"What-if" projections are made by plugging different percentages or sales figures into the first part of the worksheet and instantly seeing what the effect is on the running balance.

FIGURE 8–12 Cashflow Worksheet 1

	A	B	C	D
		JANUARY	FEBRUARY	MARCH
1		JANUARY	FEBRUARY	MARCH
2	INCOME 1	$4,530.00	$6,670.00	$8,500.00
3	INCOME 2	$7,500.00	$7,200.00	$0.00
4	INCOME 3	$3,000.00	$2,560.00	$5,000.00
5				
6	TOTALS	$15,030.00	$16,430.00	$13,500.00
7				
8		30 DAYS	60 DAYS	90 DAYS
9		20%	60%	20%
10				
11	CASH RECEIPTS:	$3,006.00	$12,304.00	$15,564.00
12				
13	RECEIVABLES:	$12,024.00	$16,150.00	$14,086.00

FIGURE 8–13 Cashflow Worksheet 2

	F	G	H	I	J
1					
2	DATE	DESCRIPTION	RECEIPTS	DISBURSEMENTS	BALANCE
3	JAN			OPENING:	$2,200.00
4	1-1	*FROM CASHFLOW'*	$1,503.00		$3,703.00
5					$3,703.00
6	1-3	SALARIES		$1,805.00	$1,898.00
7					$1,898.00
8	1-10	INSURANCE		$400.00	$1,498.00
9					$1,498.00
10					$1,498.00
11	1-12	SUPPLIES		$1,200.00	$298.00
12					$298.00
13					$298.00
14	1-15	*FROM CASHFLOW'*	$1,503.00		$1,801.00
15					$1,801.00
16					$1,801.00
17	1-20	SALARIES		$1,805.00	($4.00)
18					($4.00)
19					($4.00)
20	1-25	UTILITIES		$750.00	($754.00)
21					($754.00)
22					($754.00)
23					($754.00)
24	1-30	RENT		$2,000.00	($2,754.00)
25	FEB				($2,754.00)
26	2-1	*FROM CASHFLOW'*	$6,152.00		$3,398.00
27					$3,398.00
28	2-3	SALARIES		$1,805.00	$1,593.00
29					$1,593.00
30	2-10	INSURANCE		$400.00	$1,193.00
31					$1,193.00
32					$1,193.00
33	2-12	SUPPLIES		$1,200.00	($7.00)
34					($7.00)
35					($7.00)
36	2-15	*FROM CASHFLOW'*	$6,152.00		$6,145.00
37					$6,145.00
38	2-20	SALARIES		$1,805.00	$4,340.00
39					$4,340.00
40					$4,340.00
41	2-25	UTILITIES		$750.00	$3,590.00
42					$3,590.00
43					$3,590.00
44					$3,590.00
45					$3,590.00
46	2-28	RENT		$2,000.00	$1,590.00
47	MAR				$1,590.00
48	3-1	*FROM CASHFLOW'*	$7,782.00		$9,372.00
49					$9,372.00
50	3-3	SALARIES		$805.00	$8,567.00
51					$8,567.00
52	3-10	INSURANCE		$400.00	$8,167.00
53					$8,167.00
54					$8,167.00
55	3-12	SUPPLIES		$1,200.00	$6,967.00
56					$6,967.00
57					$6,967.00
58	3-15	*FROM CASHFLOW'*	$7,782.00		$14,749.00
59					$14,749.00
60	3-20	SALARIES		$1,805.00	$12,944.00
61					$12,944.00

FIGURE 8–14 Cashflow Worksheet 3

	F	G	H	I	J
62					$12,944.00
63	3-25	UTILITIES		$750.00	$12,194.00
64					$12,194.00
65					$12,194.00
66					$12,194.00
67					$12,194.00
68	3-30	RENT		$2,000.00	$10,194.00

Constructing the Model

Open a worksheet and clear away the gridlines with the "Display" selection on the "Options" menu. Select column A and widen the column to 14.85. Column F should be set to 4, and column G to 28.28. The other columns can remain at their standard width of 10. Select cells B8:C9 and add an outlined border with the "Border" selection on the "Format" menu. Select cells F2:J2 and outline them also. Now select cell ranges F4:J24, F26:J46, and F48:J68 (multiple selections are made by holding down the Command key when entering the additional ranges). Format these cells with complete borders by checking off everything on the "Border" menu.

Now the headings can be entered as per the illustration. They are to be boldfaced with the "Style" selection on the "Format" menu. Some are centered, and some are not—use the illustration as your guide. The headings at H2:J2 seem to be in three different cells, but actually the words "RECEIPTS DISBURSEMENTS BALANCE" are all entered into cell H2. In this manner, the column widths can be narrower than the labels that head them. We kept these columns narrow so that the entire cashflow timetable could be viewed on the screen. Notice that the headings "FROM CASHFLOW" are italicized. This is to differentiate them from entries, and they should appear on the blank (unfilled in) "CASHFLOW" worksheet.

Now select cell J3 and ranges H4:J68, B2:D6, and B11:D13. Format these as dollars and cents with the "Number" selection on the "Format" menu. Select cells B9:D9 and format these as percentages with the same selection as above. You will need to scroll down one screen to find the percentage formats.

Now we will enter the formulas (see Figures 8–15, 8–16, and 8–17). Select cell B6 and enter the formula as illustrated. Select

FIGURE 8–15 Cashflow Formulas Worksheet 1

	A	B	C	D
1		JANUARY	FEBRUARY	MARCH
2	INCOME 1			
3	INCOME 2			
4	INCOME 3			
5				
6	TOTALS	=SUM(B2:B4)	=SUM(C2:C4)	=SUM(D2:D4)
7				
8		30 DAYS	60 DAYS	90 DAYS
9				=1-C9-B9
10				
11	CASH RECEIPTS:	=B9*B6	=(B9*C6)+(C9*B6)	=(B9*D6)+(C9*C6)+(D9*B6)
12				
13	RECEIVABLES:	=B6-B11	=(B6+C6)-(B11+C11)	=(D6+C6+B6)-(B11+C11+D11)

cells B6:D6 and choose "Fill Right" from the "Edit" menu to enter formulas into these cells. The formulas in cells D9, B11:D11, and B13:D13 must all be typed in by hand—they cannot be filled. Likewise for cells H4, H14, H26, H36, H48, and H58. After you have typed in the formulas for these cells, your work is nearly over. Select J4, type in the formula as illustrated, select cells J4:J68, and fill these by choosing "Fill Down" from the "Edit" menu.

Using the Cashflow Worksheet

Enter projected sales from three separate profit centers for three months in cells B2:D4. Enter projected cash receipt percentages into cells B9:C9. Cell D9 is calculated by finding the remainder. What these numbers signify is that, for example, 20 percent of your receivables will arrive within 30 days, 60 percent will arrive within 60 days, and the remaining 20 percent will arrive within 90 days. When these numbers have been entered, your actual cash receipts for each month are calculated and displayed in cells B11:D11 and your receivables are displayed in cells B13:D13.

Now scroll over to the timetable. Columns F through J should fit perfectly on the screen. You'll see that the figures from the first section are transferred over and entered under receipts. In the example, each month's receipts are divided in half and entered on the 1st and 15th. This can easily be altered if necessary.

Enter all known disbursements for the three-month period as per the illustration. In column J you will see your running balance for the period.

FIGURE 8–16 Cashflow Formulas Worksheet 2

	F	G	H	I	J
1					
2	DATE	DESCRIPTION	RECEIPTS	DISBI	
3	JAN			OPENING:	
4	1-1	*FROM CASHFLOW'*	=B11/2		=J3+H4-I4
5					=J4+H5-I5
6					=J5+H6-I6
7					=J6+H7-I7
8					=J7+H8-I8
9					=J8+H9-I9
10					=J9+H10-I10
11					=J10+H11-I11
12					=J11+H12-I12
13					=J12+H13-I13
14	1-15	*FROM CASHFLOW'*	=B11/2		=J13+H14-I14
15					=J14+H15-I15
16					=J15+H16-I16
17					=J16+H17-I17
18					=J17+H18-I18
19					=J18+H19-I19
20					=J19+H20-I20
21					=J20+H21-I21
22					=J21+H22-I22
23					=J22+H23-I23
24					=J23+H24-I24
25	FEB				=J24+H25-I25
26	2-1	*FROM CASHFLOW'*	=C11/2		=J25+H26-I26
27					=J26+H27-I27
28					=J27+H28-I28
29					=J28+H29-I29
30		·			=J29+H30-I30
31					=J30+H31-I31
32					=J31+H32-I32
33					=J32+H33-I33
34					=J33+H34-I34
35					=J34+H35-I35
36	2-15	*FROM CASHFLOW'*	=C11/2		=J35+H36-I36
37					=J36+H37-I37
38					=J37+H38-I38
39					=J38+H39-I39
40					=J39+H40-I40
41					=J40+H41-I41
42					=J41+H42-I42
43					=J42+H43-I43
44					=J43+H44-I44
45					=J44+H45-I45
46					=J45+H46-I46
47	MAR				=J46+H47-I47
48	3-1	*FROM CASHFLOW'*	=D11/2		=J47+H48-I48
49					=J48+H49-I49
50					=J49+H50-I50
51					=J50+H51-I51
52					=J51+H52-I52
53					=J52+H53-I53
54					=J53+H54-I54
55					=J54+H55-I55

FIGURE 8–17 Cashflow Formulas Worksheet 3

	F	G	H	I	J
56					=J55+H56-I56
57					=J56+H57-I57
58	3-15	*FROM CASHFLOW*	=D11/2		=J57+H58-I58
59					=J58+H59-I59
60					=J59+H60-I60
61					=J60+H61-I61
62					=J61+H62-I62
63					=J62+H63-I63
64					=J63+H64-I64
65					=J64+H65-I65
66					=J65+H66-I66
67					=J66+H67-I67
68					=J67+H68-I68

Now you can perform "what-if" calculations. Go back to the first section of the worksheet and size the window to include only rows 1–9 and only columns A–D. Drag this window to the upper-center part of your screen. Now select the "New Window" option from the "Window" menu. Size this window to include only columns F–J and only about seven rows. Now position this window at the bottom center of your screen. You should be able to see all the way down to row 9 on the top window. You can now scroll the bottom window to whatever rows are pertinent, and you can change the entries in the top window to see what effect this has on your cashflow.

TRACKING ACCOUNTS RECEIVABLE

Purpose

The model shown in Figure 8–18 tracks the pattern of your receivables. You enter the date on which payment is received, the date of the original invoice, and the amount paid. The "RECEIVABLES" worksheet calculates how many days it took to receive payment and what percentage of your receivables arrive in 30, 60, 90, and over 90 days. This information can be used to project cashflow (enter the percentages into the "CASHFLOW" worksheet) and to time disbursements.

FIGURE 8–18 Receivables Worksheet

	A	B	C	D	E	F	G	H	I
1									
2									
3	DATE	AMOUNT	INV. DATE	DAYS	CASH	30	60	90	90+
4		$8,161.51			14.76%	37.15%	18.66%	8.34%	21.08%
5	2/2/86	$205.00	12/30/85	34			2.51%		
6	2/4/86	$400.00	11/22/85	74				4.90%	
7	2/7/86	$650.00	2/7/86	0	7.96%				
8	2/8/86	$250.00	1/24/86	15		3.06%			
9	2/8/86	$653.70	1/8/86	31			8.01%		
10	2/10/86	$850.70	11/8/85	94					10.42%
11	2/12/86	$230.44	1/7/86	36			2.82%		
12	2/14/86	$970.00	2/2/86	12		11.89%			
13	2/17/86	$433.70	1/3/86	45			5.31%		
14	2/19/86	$554.70	2/18/86	1	6.80%				
15	2/19/86	$870.00	11/4/85	107					10.66%
16	2/21/86	$110.80	2/2/86	19		1.36%			
17	2/24/86	$950.90	2/16/86	8		11.65%			
18	2/27/86	$750.67	2/2/86	25		9.20%			
19	2/28/86	$280.90	11/30/85	90				3.44%	
20									
21									
22									
23									
24									
25									
26	SUM:	$8,161.51		TOTALS:	14.76%	37.15%	18.66%	8.34%	21.08%

Constructing the Model

On a new worksheet, set the column widths (with that selection on the "Format" menu) as follows: A:8, B:8, C:8, D:4, E:6, F:6, G:6, H:6, and I:6. You should be able to see columns A through I in their entirety on your screen. If you can't, you can enlarge the window to fill the entire screen. From the "Options" menu, select "Display" and clear away the gridlines by unchecking that selection. Select the following cells and ranges simultaneously by using the multiple selection technique (hold down the Command key while clicking additional cells): A3:I3, B4, E4:I4, B26, and E26:I26. From the "Format" menu, choose "Border" and check off all of the selections. Type in the headings as illustrated. Using selections from the "Format" menu, boldface the headings and center-align all of them except for the following: "SUM" in A26 is right-aligned, and "TOTALS:" is in C26 with nine spaces preceding it ("   TOTALS") so that it will line up properly.

Select cells B4:B26 and format them as dollars and cents by choosing the bottom selection from the "Numbers" submenu, which in turn is found under the "Format" menu. Select cell ranges A5:A25 and C5:C25 and format them as dates by choosing mm/dd/yy, also from the "Numbers" submenu. (You'll have to scroll down one screen to find this selection.) Now select cells E4:I26 and format these as percentages by choosing "0.00%" (also down one screen) on the "Numbers" submenu.

Entering the formulas looks like a lot of typing, but through the miracle of the "Fill" command it is actually quite simple (see Figures 8–19, 8–20, and 8–21). Select B4 and enter the formula illustrated. Select E4 and enter its illustrated formula; then select cells E4:I4 and choose "Fill Right" from the "Edit" menu. Now select cell D5, enter the illustrated formula, select cells D5:D25,

FIGURE 8–19 Receivables Formulas Worksheet 1

	A	B	C	D	E
1					
2					
3	DATE	AMOUNT	INV. DATE	DAYS	CASH
4		=B26			=E26
5				=IF(A5>0,A5-C5,"")	=IF(AND(D5<2,B5>0),B5/$B$26,"")
6				=IF(A6>0,A6-C6,"")	=IF(AND(D6<2,B6>0),B6/$B$26,"")
7				=IF(A7>0,A7-C7,"")	=IF(AND(D7<2,B7>0),B7/$B$26,"")
8				=IF(A8>0,A8-C8,"")	=IF(AND(D8<2,B8>0),B8/$B$26,"")
9				=IF(A9>0,A9-C9,"")	=IF(AND(D9<2,B9>0),B9/$B$26,"")
10				=IF(A10>0,A10-C10,"")	=IF(AND(D10<2,B10>0),B10/$B$26,"")
11				=IF(A11>0,A11-C11,"")	=IF(AND(D11<2,B11>0),B11/$B$26,"")
12				=IF(A12>0,A12-C12,"")	=IF(AND(D12<2,B12>0),B12/$B$26,"")
13				=IF(A13>0,A13-C13,"")	=IF(AND(D13<2,B13>0),B13/$B$26,"")
14				=IF(A14>0,A14-C14,"")	=IF(AND(D14<2,B14>0),B14/$B$26,"")
15				=IF(A15>0,A15-C15,"")	=IF(AND(D15<2,B15>0),B15/$B$26,"")
16				=IF(A16>0,A16-C16,"")	=IF(AND(D16<2,B16>0),B16/$B$26,"")
17				=IF(A17>0,A17-C17,"")	=IF(AND(D17<2,B17>0),B17/$B$26,"")
18				=IF(A18>0,A18-C18,"")	=IF(AND(D18<2,B18>0),B18/$B$26,"")
19				=IF(A19>0,A19-C19,"")	=IF(AND(D19<2,B19>0),B19/$B$26,"")
20				=IF(A20>0,A20-C20,"")	=IF(AND(D20<2,B20>0),B20/$B$26,"")
21				=IF(A21>0,A21-C21,"")	=IF(AND(D21<2,B21>0),B21/$B$26,"")
22				=IF(A22>0,A22-C22,"")	=IF(AND(D22<2,B22>0),B22/$B$26,"")
23				=IF(A23>0,A23-C23,"")	=IF(AND(D23<2,B23>0),B23/$B$26,"")
24				=IF(A24>0,A24-C24,"")	=IF(AND(D24<2,B24>0),B24/$B$26,"")
25				=IF(A25>0,A25-C25,"")	=IF(AND(D25<2,B25>0),B25/$B$26,"")
26	SUM:	=SUM(B5	TO1		=SUM(E5:E25)

FIGURE 8–20 Receivables Formulas Worksheet 2

	F	G
1		
2		
3	30	60
4	=F26	=G26
5	=IF(AND(D5>1,D5<31),B5/$B$26,"")	=IF(AND(D5>30,D5<61),B5/$B$26,"")
6	=IF(AND(D6>1,D6<31),B6/$B$26,"")	=IF(AND(D6>30,D6<61),B6/$B$26,"")
7	=IF(AND(D7>1,D7<31),B7/$B$26,"")	=IF(AND(D7>30,D7<61),B7/$B$26,"")
8	=IF(AND(D8>1,D8<31),B8/$B$26,"")	=IF(AND(D8>30,D8<61),B8/$B$26,"")
9	=IF(AND(D9>1,D9<31),B9/$B$26,"")	=IF(AND(D9>30,D9<61),B9/$B$26,"")
10	=IF(AND(D10>1,D10<31),B10/$B$26,"")	=IF(AND(D10>30,D10<61),B10/$B$26,"")
11	=IF(AND(D11>1,D11<31),B11/$B$26,"")	=IF(AND(D11>30,D11<61),B11/$B$26,"")
12	=IF(AND(D12>1,D12<31),B12/$B$26,"")	=IF(AND(D12>30,D12<61),B12/$B$26,"")
13	=IF(AND(D13>1,D13<31),B13/$B$26,"")	=IF(AND(D13>30,D13<61),B13/$B$26,"")
14	=IF(AND(D14>1,D14<31),B14/$B$26,"")	=IF(AND(D14>30,D14<61),B14/$B$26,"")
15	=IF(AND(D15>1,D15<31),B15/$B$26,"")	=IF(AND(D15>30,D15<61),B15/$B$26,"")
16	=IF(AND(D16>1,D16<31),B16/$B$26,"")	=IF(AND(D16>30,D16<61),B16/$B$26,"")
17	=IF(AND(D17>1,D17<31),B17/$B$26,"")	=IF(AND(D17>30,D17<61),B17/$B$26,"")
18	=IF(AND(D18>1,D18<31),B18/$B$26,"")	=IF(AND(D18>30,D18<61),B18/$B$26,"")
19	=IF(AND(D19>1,D19<31),B19/$B$26,"")	=IF(AND(D19>30,D19<61),B19/$B$26,"")
20	=IF(AND(D20>1,D20<31),B20/$B$26,"")	=IF(AND(D20>30,D20<61),B20/$B$26,"")
21	=IF(AND(D21>1,D21<31),B21/$B$26,"")	=IF(AND(D21>30,D21<61),B21/$B$26,"")
22	=IF(AND(D22>1,D22<31),B22/$B$26,"")	=IF(AND(D22>30,D22<61),B22/$B$26,"")
23	=IF(AND(D23>1,D23<31),B23/$B$26,"")	=IF(AND(D23>30,D23<61),B23/$B$26,"")
24	=IF(AND(D24>1,D24<31),B24/$B$26,"")	=IF(AND(D24>30,D24<61),B24/$B$26,"")
25	=IF(AND(D25>1,D25<31),B25/$B$26,"")	=IF(AND(D25>30,D25<61),B25/$B$26,"")
26	=SUM(F5:F25)	=SUM(G5:G25)

and fill these by choosing "Fill Down" from the "Edit" menu. Repeat these steps by entering the formulas into E5, F5, G5, H5, and I5. Choose cells E5:I25 and fill down.

All that remains now is row 26. Enter the illustrated formula into cells B26 and E26. Select cells E26:I26 and fill right.

The formulas may seem overly complex for the job they are doing — particularly the formulas that contain "IF" and "AND." It should be remembered, however, that these are written not only to produce the correct value but to eliminate the display of zeros in blank cells.

Using the Receivables Model

The "RECEIVABLES" worksheet can be set up to accommodate any length of time. In the example it is used during a one-month period. As payments arrive, enter them onto the worksheet. List first the current date, then the amount received, then the date of

FIGURE 8–21 Receivables Formulas Worksheet 3

	H	I
1		
2		
3	90	90+
4	=H26	=I26
5	=IF(AND(D5>60,D5<91),B5/$B$26,"")	=IF(AND(D5>90,B5>0),B5/$B$26,"")
6	=IF(AND(D6>60,D6<91),B6/$B$26,"")	=IF(AND(D6>90,B6>0),B6/$B$26,"")
7	=IF(AND(D7>60,D7<91),B7/$B$26,"")	=IF(AND(D7>90,B7>0),B7/$B$26,"")
8	=IF(AND(D8>60,D8<91),B8/$B$26,"")	=IF(AND(D8>90,B8>0),B8/$B$26,"")
9	=IF(AND(D9>60,D9<91),B9/$B$26,"")	=IF(AND(D9>90,B9>0),B9/$B$26,"")
10	=IF(AND(D10>60,D10<91),B10/$B$26,"")	=IF(AND(D10>90,B10>0),B10/$B$26,"")
11	=IF(AND(D11>60,D11<91),B11/$B$26,"")	=IF(AND(D11>90,B11>0),B11/$B$26,"")
12	=IF(AND(D12>60,D12<91),B12/$B$26,"")	=IF(AND(D12>90,B12>0),B12/$B$26,"")
13	=IF(AND(D13>60,D13<91),B13/$B$26,"")	=IF(AND(D13>90,B13>0),B13/$B$26,"")
14	=IF(AND(D14>60,D14<91),B14/$B$26,"")	=IF(AND(D14>90,B14>0),B14/$B$26,"")
15	=IF(AND(D15>60,D15<91),B15/$B$26,"")	=IF(AND(D15>90,B15>0),B15/$B$26,"")
16	=IF(AND(D16>60,D16<91),B16/$B$26,"")	=IF(AND(D16>90,B16>0),B16/$B$26,"")
17	=IF(AND(D17>60,D17<91),B17/$B$26,"")	=IF(AND(D17>90,B17>0),B17/$B$26,"")
18	=IF(AND(D18>60,D18<91),B18/$B$26,"")	=IF(AND(D18>90,B18>0),B18/$B$26,"")
19	=IF(AND(D19>60,D19<91),B19/$B$26,"")	=IF(AND(D19>90,B19>0),B19/$B$26,"")
20	=IF(AND(D20>60,D20<91),B20/$B$26,"")	=IF(AND(D20>90,B20>0),B20/$B$26,"")
21	=IF(AND(D21>60,D21<91),B21/$B$26,"")	=IF(AND(D21>90,B21>0),B21/$B$26,"")
22	=IF(AND(D22>60,D22<91),B22/$B$26,"")	=IF(AND(D22>90,B22>0),B22/$B$26,"")
23	=IF(AND(D23>60,D23<91),B23/$B$26,"")	=IF(AND(D23>90,B23>0),B23/$B$26,"")
24	=IF(AND(D24>60,D24<91),B24/$B$26,"")	=IF(AND(D24>90,B24>0),B24/$B$26,"")
25	=IF(AND(D25>60,D25<91),B25/$B$26,"")	=IF(AND(D25>90,B25>0),B25/$B$26,"")
26	=SUM(H5:H25)	=SUM(I5:I25)

the original invoice. The worksheet will calculate the number of days it took to collect, and this number will appear in the Days column. The percentage in the same row as the entry will appear in the appropriate column to reflect the broader collection period: Cash (within 1 day), within 30 days, within 60 days, within 90 days, and over 90 days. The percentage number itself reflects what percentage of the total payments received thus far this individual entry represents. In the boxes at the top and bottom of the columns are the total percentages for the columns. This tells you, for example, that 15 percent of your sales was cash, 37 percent was received within 30 days, 19 percent was received within 60 days, 8 percent was received within 90 days, and 21 percent took over 90 days to collect.

These data can be very useful to project cash flow and plan disbursement timing. In fact, these numbers can be plugged right into the "CASHFLOW" worksheet.

DETERMINING SALES PRODUCTIVITY

Purpose

In any type of business that involves a sales force, it is useful to be able to determine the productivity of the salespeople at a glance. The model shown in Figures 8–22 and 8–23 allows the user to quickly determine both total production by month and total production by salesperson by years. In addition, it automatically calculates the sales commission paid.

Constructing the Model

Open a new worksheet. Select column widths depending on the size of the names used. Insert the first date in cell A2 (using one of the standard Excel formats as indicated here); then fill downward for as many dates as needed by highlighting and using the "Data, Series" command.

Fill in the names and titles that are appropriate to your application or use those shown here. Finally, fill in the formulas as indicated (see Figures 8–24, 8–25, and 8–26). The sales commission formula (row 16) currently shows a 10 percent commission. This

---

FIGURE 8–22   Sales Production Worksheet 1

	A	B	C	D	E	F	G	H
1		Allan	Bill	Francis	Henry	Prudence	Wilma	Total Sales
2	Jan-86	$3,657	$4,066	$5,384	$2,546	$14,347	$10,968	$40,968
3	Feb-86	$6,859	$4,365	$7,495	$3,564	$13,654	$6,574	$42,511
4	Mar-86	$4,588	$4,586	$5,893	$4,538	$14,327	$5,342	$39,274
5	Apr-86	$8,977	$4,623	$9,463	$4,987	$11,308	$7,854	$47,212
6	May-86	$9,023	$4,677	$12,086	$5,987	$10,964	$9,833	$52,570
7	Jun-86	$10,045	$4,796	$11,960	$2,314	$8,624	$9,333	$47,072
8	Jul-86	$2,456	$4,986	$5,467	$3,452	$14,002	$5,426	$35,789
9	Aug-86	$2,768	$5,204	$5,367	$2,314	$11,546	$2,109	$29,308
10	Sep-86	$4,778	$5,300	$7,586	$2,318	$12,657	$469	$33,108
11	Oct-86	$6,987	$5,467	$8,342	$0	$13,556	$4,879	$39,231
12	Nov-86	$9,305	$5,471	$10,673	$0	$12,765	$7,099	$45,313
13	Dec-86	$9,986	$5,682	$10,967	$0	$11,436	$8,932	$47,003
14								
15	Total Sales	$79,429	$59,223	$100,683	$32,020	$149,186	$78,818	$499,359
16	Commission	$7,943	$5,922	$10,068	$3,202	$14,919	$7,882	
17								

FIGURE 8–23 Sales Production Worksheet 2

	I
1	**Commission**
2	$4,097
3	$4,251
4	$3,927
5	$4,721
6	$5,257
7	$4,707
8	$3,579
9	$2,931
10	$3,311
11	$3,923
12	$4,531
13	$4,700
14	
15	
16	$49,936
17	

FIGURE 8–24 Sales Production Formulas Worksheet 1

	A	B	C	D
1		Allan	Bill	Francis
2	29951			
3	29982			
4	30010			
5	30041			
6	30071			
7	30102			
8	30132			
9	30163			
10	30194			
11	30224			
12	30255			
13	30285			
14				
15	Total Sales	=SUM(B2:B13)	=SUM(C2:C13)	=SUM(D2:D13)
16	Commission	=0.1*B15	=0.1*C15	=0.1*D15
17				

can, of course, be changed to any commission rate desired. (The formulas need not all be filled in by hand—just type the first one, then use the "Fill" command to fill the remaining cells.)

FIGURE 8–25 Sales Production Formulas Worksheet 2

	E	F	G	H
1	Henry	Prudence	Vilma	Total Sales
2				=SUM(B2:G2)
3				=SUM(B3:G3)
4				=SUM(B4:G4)
5				=SUM(B5:G5)
6				=SUM(B6:G6)
7				=SUM(B7:G7)
8				=SUM(B8:G8)
9				=SUM(B9:G9)
10				=SUM(B10:G10)
11				=SUM(B11:G11)
12				=SUM(B12:G12)
13				=SUM(B13:G13)
14				
15	=SUM(E2:E13)	=SUM(F2:F13)	=SUM(G2:G13)	=SUM(H2:H13)
16	=0.1*E15	=0.1*F15	=0.1*G15	
17				

FIGURE 8–26 Sales Production Formulas Worksheet 3

	I
1	Commission
2	=0.1*H2
3	=0.1*H3
4	=0.1*H4
5	=0.1*H5
6	=0.1*H6
7	=0.1*H7
8	=0.1*H8
9	=0.1*H9
10	=0.1*H10
11	=0.1*H11
12	=0.1*H12
13	=0.1*H13
14	
15	
16	=SUM(I2:I13)
17	

FIGURE 8–27   Sales Chart 1

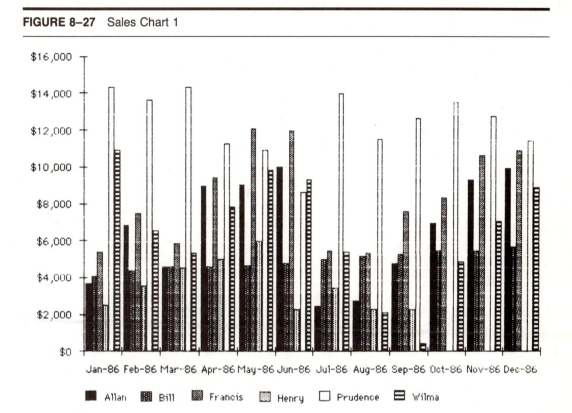

Using the Model

Insert the sales production figures for each salesperson. The model will automatically calculate total sales and total commissions by month on the right. It will automatically calculate total sales and commissions *by salesperson* at the bottom.

Charting

The sales productivity application lends itself to graphic description. The charts shown in Figures 8–27, 8–28, and 8–29 were developed using the previous worksheet data. (See the section "Creating a Chart" in Chapter 13.)

FIGURE 8–28 Sales Chart 2

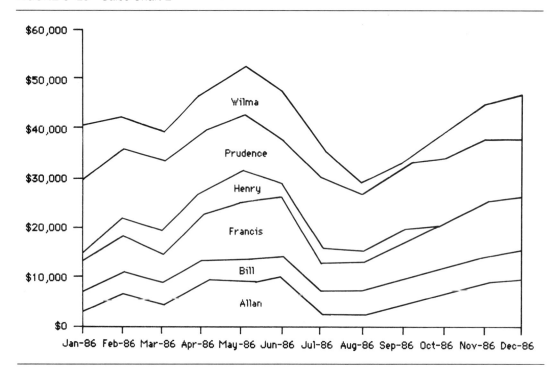

FIGURE 8–29 Sales Chart 3

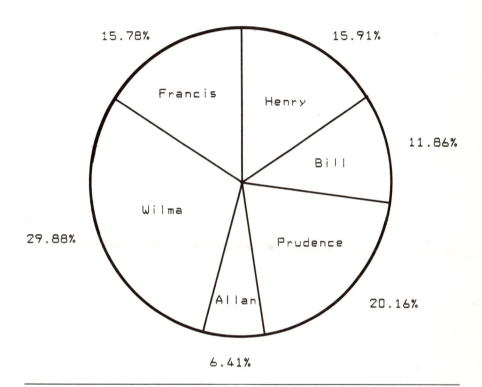

Total Commissions

CHAPTER 9

Financial Statements

Financial statements have two uses. First, they allow us to see how well our business is doing at any given time. Second, they allow us to present that information to others. In this chapter we will construct four kinds of financial statements:

Balance Sheet
Profit/Loss (Income) Sheet
Operating Expenses Sheet
Cost of Goods Sold Sheet

BALANCE SHEET

Purpose

A standard financial balance sheet sums up a company's position as of a certain date. It is divided into two sections, assets and liabilities. The "bottom line," or totals, for these two sections should agree, or balance. The balance sheet in Figures 9–1 and 9–2 is designed to show two years.

Constructing the Model

In this case constructing the model is a cut-and-dried process consisting of sizing the columns (A=31.5, B=14, and C=14) and entering the formulas (see Figures 9–3 and 9–4). You'll probably want to alter the labels to fit your own business, but in the begin-

FIGURE 9–1 Balance Sheet 1

	A	B	C
1	WIDGET COMPANY		
2	Balance Sheet		
3	On 12/31/85 & 12/31/86	1985	1986
4			
5	Assets		
6			
7			
8			
9			
10	Current Assets		
11	Cash	$115,000.00	$125,000.00
12	Marketable Securities	$55,000.00	$47,321.00
13	Certificates of Deposit	$70,000.00	$110,000.00
14	Accounts Receivable	$105,555.00	$99,177.00
15	Inventory	$329,211.00	$317,875.00
16	Prepaid Expenses	$7,800.00	$3,000.00
17	Other	$5,900.00	$221.00
18			
19	Total Current Assets	$688,466.00	$702,594.00
20			
21	Property and Equipment		
22	Land and Buildings	$135,670.00	$135,670.00
23	Furniture and Equipment	$47,900.00	$53,600.00
24	Machinery	$55,920.00	$55,920.00
25	Leasehold Improvements	$0.00	$21,200.00
26			
27	Total Property & Equipment	$239,490.00	$266,390.00
28			
29	Accumulated Depreciation & Amortization	$67,500.00	$92,870.00
30			
31	Net Property & Equipment	$171,990.00	$173,520.00
32			
33	Other Assets	$450.00	$300.00
34			
35	Total Assets	$860,906.00	$876,414.00
36			
37			
38			
39			
40			
41			
42			
43			
44			
45			
46			
47			
48		1985	1986
49			
50			
51	Current Liabilities		
52	Notes Payable	$121,450.00	$124,870.00
53	Current Obligations Under Capital Leases	$0.00	$15,467.00
54	Taxes Payable	$9,055.00	$12,366.00
55	Accounts Payable	$197,870.00	$203,965.00

FIGURE 9–2 Balance Sheet 2

	A	B	C
56	Accrued Salaries and Wages	$57,643.00	$61,332.00
57	Other Accrued Expense	$29,900.00	$24,540.00
58	Other Current Liabilities	$700.00	$0.00
59			
60	Total Current Liabilities	$416,618.00	$442,540.00
61			
62			
63	Long-Term Debt	$245,822.00	$235,790.00
64			
65	Other Liabilities	$7,000.00	$2,500.00
66			
67	Total Liabilities	$669,440.00	$680,830.00
68			
69	Stockholders' Equity		
70	Common Stock	$75,000.00	$75,000.00
71	Retained Earnings	$116,466.00	$120,584.00
72			
73	Total Stockholders' Equity	$191,466.00	$195,584.00
74			
75	Total Liabilities and Equity	$860,906.00	$876,414.00

ning it might be helpful for you to enter the illustrated labels in order to comprehend the financial relationships established.

Using the Balance Sheet

Simply enter figures into all cells that don't already contain formulas. The sheet will automatically do all the subtotaling, totaling, and referring for you.

PROFIT/LOSS (INCOME) SHEET

Purpose

The income sheet, also referred to as a profit/loss sheet, shows how much money a company took in over a given period, usually a year. It lists expenses, such as operating expenses, interest on loans, and taxes, and calculates a net profit figure. The model shown in Figure 9–5 refers to other worksheets, namely "COST_OF_GOODS_ SOLD" and "OPERATING_EXPENSES," for certain figures. You

FIGURE 9–3 Balance Sheet Formulas 1

	A	B	C
1	WIDGET COMPANY		
2	Balance Sheet		
3	On 12/31/85 & 12/31/86	1985	1986
4			
5	Assets		
6			
7			
8			
9			
10	Current Assets		
11	Cash		
12	Marketable Securities		
13	Certificates of Deposit		
14	Accounts Receivable		
15	Inventory		
16	Prepaid Expenses		
17	Other		
18			
19	Total Current Assets	=SUM($B$11:$B$17)	=SUM($C$11:$C$17)
20			
21	Property and Equipment		
22	Land and Buildings		
23	Furniture and Equipment		
24	Machinery		
25	Leasehold Improvements		
26			
27	Total Property & Equipment	=SUM(B22:B25)	=SUM(C22:C25)
28			
29	Accumulated Depreciation &		
30			
31	Net Property & Equipment	=B27-B29	=C27-C29
32			
33	Other Assets		
34			
35	Total Assets	=$B$19+$B$31+B	=$C$19+$C$31+C
36			
37			
38			
39			
40			
41			
42			
43			
44			
45			
46			
47			
48		1985	1986
49			
50			
51	Current Liabilities		
52	Notes Payable		
53	Current Obligations Under (		
54	Taxes Payable		

FIGURE 9–4 Balance Sheet Formulas 2

	A	B	C
55	Accounts Payable		
56	Accrued Salaries and Wages		
57	Other Accrued Expense		
58	Other Current Liabilities		
59			
60	Total Current Liabilities	=SUM(B52:B58)	=SUM(C52:C58)
61			
62			
63	Long-Term Debt		
64			
65	Other Liabilities		
66			
67	Total Liabilities	=B60+B63+B65	=C60+C63+C65
68			
69	Stockholders' Equity		
70	Common Stock		
71	Retained Earnings		
72			
73	Total Stockholders' Equity	=B70+B71	=C70+C71
74			
75	Total Liabilities and Equity	=B67+B73	=C67+C73

may replace the formulas and enter these figures directly if you prefer not to open the other worksheets.

Constructing the Model

Like some of its linked cousins, this worksheet is easy to construct: simply size the columns (A=30, B=14, and C=14), format the appropriate cells for dollars and cents, boldface or center-align as per the illustration, and enter the formulas (see Figure 9–6). Naturally, you will want to change some of the labels to suit your particular business, but be careful to update the formulas and referrals.

Using the Income Sheet

Enter figures into cells that do not already have formulas in them. The worksheet will automatically do all subtotaling, totaling, and referring for you. Linked worksheets need to be open simultaneously in order to update referrals.

FIGURE 9–5   Income Sheet

	A	B	C
1	**WIDGET COMPANY**		
2	Statement of Income		
3	For Years Ended 12/31/85 & 12/31/86		
4			
5		1985	1986
6			
7			
8	Revenues		
9	Gross Sales	$1,045,000.00	$1,256,300.00
10	Less: Returns and Allowances	$1,000.00	$0.00
11	Net Sales	$1,044,000.00	$1,256,300.00
12	Interest on Deposits	$3,700.00	$4,630.00
13	Total Revenues	$1,047,700.00	$1,260,930.00
14			
15			
16	Cost of Goods Sold	$740,447.00	$787,155.00
17			
18	Net Revenue	$307,253.00	$473,775.00
19			
20	Operating Expenses	$356,600.00	$375,335.00
21			
22	Other Income/Expense	$13,450.00	$37,540.00
23			
24	Profit Before Taxes	($62,797.00)	$60,900.00
25			
26	Income Taxes	$0.00	$29,232.00
27			
28	Net Income	($62,797.00)	$31,668.00

OPERATING EXPENSES SHEET

Purpose

The worksheet shown in Figure 9–7 details all of the expenses that occurred as a result of operating a business within a given time period, usually a year. This particular model is designed to illustrate two years, as are all of the linked worksheets in this chapter.

Constructing the Model

Easy as pie. Set the column widths to A=32.4, B=14, and C=14. Format columns B and C for dollars and cents except for where

FIGURE 9–6 Income Sheet Formulas

	A	B	C
1	WIDGET COMPANY		
2	Statement of Income		
3	For Years Ended 12/31/85 & 12/31/86		
4			
5		1985	1986
6			
7			
8	Revenues		
9	Gross Sales		
10	Less: Returns and Allowances		
11	Net Sales	=B9-B10	=C9-C10
12	Interest on Deposits		
13	Total Revenues	=B11+B12	=C11+C12
14			
15			
16	Cost of Goods Sold	=COST_OF_GOODS_SOLD!$B$22	=COST_OF_GOODS_SOLD!$C$22
17			
18	Net Revenue	=B13-B16	=C13-C16
19			
20	Operating Expenses	=OPERATING_EXPENSES!$B$25	=OPERATING_EXPENSES!$C$25
21			
22	Other Income/Expense		
23			
24	Profit Before Taxes	=B18-B20-B22	=C18-C20-C22
25			
26	Income Taxes		
27			
28	Net Income	=B24-B26	=C24-C26

the year labels go. There is only one referral on this sheet; it gets the depreciation for the current year from the "BALANCE" worksheet. This can be filled in directly if you prefer. Enter the two "SUM" formulas at the bottom, and you're ready to go (see Figure 9–8). If you should want to insert or delete cells, the "SUM" formulas will update themselves automatically as long as cells are not inserted at the top or bottom line (insert them in the middle).

Using the Worksheet

Type in the labels for your operating expenses, and type in the figures; that's all there is to it. The model will calculate the sums for you, and in the case of depreciation, look at the "BALANCE" worksheet for that figure.

FIGURE 9–7 Operating Expenses Worksheet

	A	B	C
1	**WIDGET COMPANY**		
2	Statement of Operating Expenses		
3	For the Years ending 12/31/85& 12/31/86		
4			
5		1985	1986
6			
7	Advertising and Promotion	$50,670.00	$55,754.00
8	Depreciation	$35,000.00	$25,370.00
9	Employee Benefits	$6,600.00	$7,760.00
10	Expense Accounts	$14,500.00	$15,600.00
11	Health Insurance	$3,670.00	$4,120.00
12	Insurance	$800.00	$1,200.00
13	Maintenance	$2,133.00	$3,210.00
14	Miscellaneous	$305.00	$428.00
15	Payroll Taxes	$27,142.00	$31,560.00
16	Postage	$870.00	$1,050.00
17	Professional Fees	$1,760.00	$1,869.00
18	Professional Organization Dues	$1,130.00	$1,130.00
19	Publicity Photography	$5,000.00	$7,800.00
20	Rent	$15,600.00	$15,600.00
21	Rentals	$6,670.00	$8,800.00
22	Salaries and Wages	$175,850.00	$184,584.00
23	Telephone	$8,900.00	$9,500.00
24			
25	Total Operating Expenses	$356,600.00	$375,335.00

COST OF GOODS SOLD SHEET

Purpose

The worksheet shown in Figure 9–9 calculates what it actually costs to make those widgets you make, taking into consideration such things as materials, labor, overhead, and opening and closing inventory. The example lists two separate years for comparison, and it takes the beginning inventory figure for the new year from the ending inventory figure for the previous year.

Constructing the Model

Simple. Set the column widths: A=32, B=14, and C=14. Format columns B and C as dollars and cents except for the cells contain-

FIGURE 9–8 Operating Expenses Worksheet Formulas

	A	B	C
1	WIDGET COMPANY		
2	Statement of Operating Expenses		
3	For the Years ending 12/31/85& 12/31/86		
4			
5		1985	1986
6			
7	Advertising and Promotion		
8	Depreciation		
9	Employee Benefits		
10	Expense Accounts		
11	Health Insurance		
12	Insurance		
13	Maintenence		
14	Miscellaneous		
15	Payroll Taxes		
16	Postage		
17	Professional Fees		
18	Professional Organization Dues		
19	Publicity Photography		
20	Rent		
21	Rentals		
22	Salaries and Wages		
23	Telephone		
24			
25	Total Operating Expenses	=SUM(B7:B23)	=SUM(C7:C23)

ing the year labels. Type in the headings and formulas, and you're ready to go (see Figure 9–10). If you change some of the headings, be sure to update the formulas.

Using the Cost of Goods Sold Worksheet

Type in figures for categories that do not have formulas. The worksheet will automatically do all the calculating for you.

FIGURE 9–9   Cost of Goods Sold Worksheet

	A	B	C
1	WIDGET COMPANY		
2	Statement of Costs of Goods Sold		
3	For the Years Ended 12/31/85 & 12/31/86		
4			
5		1985	1986
6			
7			
8	Beginning Inventory	$422,687.00	$411,678.00
9	Plus: Purchases	$400,345.00	$399,078.00
10	Less: Returns & Allowances	$27,567.00	$21,978.00
11			
12	Total Inventory	$795,465.00	$788,778.00
13			
14	Ending Inventory	$411,678.00	$376,958.00
15			
16	Cost of Materials	$383,787.00	$411,820.00
17			
18	Cost of Labor	$286,987.00	$299,678.00
19	Plant Overhead	$69,003.00	$75,345.00
20	Other Costs	$670.00	$312.00
21			
22	Total Cost of Goods Sold	$740,447.00	$787,155.00

FIGURE 9–10   Cost of Goods Sold Worksheet Formulas

	A	B	C
1	WIDGET COMPANY		
2	Statement of Costs of Goods Sold		
3	For the Years Ended 12/31/85 & 12/31/86		
4			
5		1985	1986
6			
7			
8	Beginning Inventory		=$B$14
9	Plus: Purchases		
10	Less: Returns & Allowances		
11			
12	Total Inventory	=B8+B9-B10	=C8+C9-C10
13			
14	Ending Inventory		
15			
16	Cost of Materials	=B12-B14	=C12-C14
17			
18	Cost of Labor		
19	Plant Overhead		
20	Other Costs		
21			
22	Total Cost of Goods Sold	=B16+B18+B19+B20	=C16+C18+C19+C20

CHAPTER 10

Data Processing Applications

Although the primary function of a spreadsheet is not data processing, Excel does allow the user to perform some basic data processing tasks. In this chapter we'll look at how a mailing list can be set up and sorted (both by zip and by alphabet).

Then we'll go on to see how we can find and extract information from a database using the mailing list we first created. Thus this chapter has two sections:

Mailing List
Finding and Extracting from a Database Management

MAILING LIST

Purpose

The worksheet shown in Figures 10–1 and 10–2 provides sorting (including sorting by zip code) and alphabetizing of a lengthy mailing list, which can later be printed out to make mailing labels or individual addresses on envelopes.

Constructing the Model

This is probably one of the easiest models to construct. Column widths can be set for any convenient width and later expanded if necessary; in the example they are set as follows: A=16, B=16, C=16, D=25, E=16, F=5, and G=5. Labels are typed into A1:G1

FIGURE 10–1   Mailing List Worksheet 1

	A	B	C	D
1				
2	**LAST**	**FIRST**	**COMPANY**	**STREET**
3	Anderson	Fred	Widget Inc.	1011 Plam Drive.
4	Bisset	Joseph		1417 Reshum Way
5	Carrol	Susan	Susan's Hardware	124 Wayland St.
6	Falk	Marvin	IBM Lookalike Inc.	34314 Neehigh Drive
7	Johnson	David		182 Grower St. #313
8	Kronbrite	Ida	Wealth Enterprises	1869 Howard Square
9	Lang	Charles	Surf Shop	18 Kalauhu St.
10	Lansberg	John	Plainname Co.	123 Main St.
11	Monery	John		888 Nomand St.
12	Smith	Sandy	Hartley Mattress	22443 Softly Drive
13	Smith	Milton	Kronbrite Photographic	1841 Coral St.

FIGURE 10–2   Mailing List Worksheet 2

	E	F	G
1			
2	**CITY**	**STATE**	**ZIP**
3	Thousand Oaks	CA	90234
4	Minneapolis	MI	23156
5	Baltimore	MD	21208
6	New York	NY	10019
7	Chicago	IL	60606
8	Arlington	VA	33112
9	Honolulu	HA	87590
10	Miami	FL	44512
11	Detroit	MI	77884
12	Seattle	WA	88665
13	Dallas	TX	44556

(feel free to alter or combine fields according to your own needs). Keep in mind that any sorting or searching will be done by fields or discrete columns—therefore, in the illustrated example, it would be difficult to sort by street names because these are combined with street numbers. Zip codes are given their own field since post offices often offer discounts for mail presorted by zip code.

After the headings have been typed in, centered, and bold-faced (the last two are done from the "Format" menu), the model is completed.

Using the Model

Although the illustrated example contains a short mailing list, the advantage of Excel lies in its handling of large, otherwise unmanageable mailing lists. Whereas with other database programs much trouble and complication may be required to change the size of a field if you run into a longer name than usual, with Excel you simply move the column over. Likewise with inserting or deleting fields (columns).

The first thing to do when the list is to be used is to select the entire list, either by starting the cursor at A3 and dragging it down to the bottom right or, if the list is too long, by selecting A3 and, with the Shift key down, selecting the bottom-right cell. All other cells in between will then be selected. Now we want to name this selection so that in the future we can use the "Formula" menu's "Goto" function. Select "Define Name" from the "Formula" menu. We named ours "MAILLIST." Once this selection has been named, you can test the function by selecting a cell at random, then using "Goto" on the "Formula" menu. When you double-click your list's name, the entire list should be selected.

Let's begin by alphabetizing the list. Select the entire list, then choose "Sort" from the "Data" menu. The first key will probably read "$A$3" (if not, type this in). Leave the choices "Rows" and "Ascending" selected (select them if this has not already been done). Fill in the second key as "$B$3." This means that if the last names are the same, Excel will go to the first names to alphabetize. Click OK. Your list will be alphabetized. Easy, huh?

Let's sort by zip code. Again, choose "Sort" from the "Data" menu. This time make "$G$3" the first key choice, "$A$3" the second key choice, and "$B$3" the third key choice. Be sure not to hit "Enter" until all three are filled in. Now the list is sorted first by zip code, then by last name, then by first name.

You can put 16,384 names on this list. If that's not enough, you can start another list next to the original one, putting A–L on one list and M–Z on another.

In addition to sorting, it is possible to find and extract with the database functions. These are covered in the next section.

FINDING AND EXTRACTING FROM A DATABASE

Purpose

An Excel database can be sorted in very specific ways, to meet certain narrow or broad criteria. The matching records can be found, extracted, deleted, or altered. For the purpose of our example, shown in Figures 10–3 and 10–4, we will continue using the mailing list from the previous example. Although the list in the example is short, the database functions would be most useful on long and cumbersome lists.

Constructing the Model

We will build on the model created for the previous example, "MAILING_LIST." Select cells A2:G2, which comprise the headings. These will be copied and pasted twice. Select "Copy" from the "Edit" menu and then select cell A15. (If your list is longer than that of the example, choose a cell a few rows below the last name on the list. Be sure to convert the following references to your new location.) Choose "Paste" from the "Edit" menu. Now select cell

---

FIGURE 10–3 Database Worksheet 1

	A	B	C	D
1				
2	LAST	FIRST	COMPANY	STREET
3	Anderson	Fred	Widget Inc.	1011 Plam Drive.
4	Bisset	Joseph		1417 Reshum Way
5	Carrol	Susan	Susan's Hardware	124 Wayland St.
6	Falk	Marvin	IBM Lookalike Inc.	34314 Neehigh Drive
7	Johnson	David		182 Grower St. #313
8	Kronbrite	Ida	Wealth Enterprises	1869 Howard Square
9	Lang	Charles	Surf Shop	18 Kalauhu St.
10	Lansberg	John	Plainname Co.	123 Main St.
11	Monery	John		888 Nomand St.
12	Smith	Sandy	Hartley Mattress	22443 Softly Drive
13	Smith	Milton	Kronbrite Photographic	1841 Coral St.
14				
15	LAST	FIRST	COMPANY	STREET
16	>F	Jo		1
17				
18	LAST	FIRST	COMPANY	STREET
19	Lansberg	John	Plainname Co.	123 Main St.
20	Monery	John		888 Nomand St.

FIGURE 10–4 Database Worksheet 2

	E	F	G
1			
2	**CITY**	**STATE**	**ZIP**
3	Thousand Oaks	CA	90234
4	Minneapolis	MI	23156
5	Baltimore	MD	21208
6	New York	NY	10019
7	Chicago	IL	60606
8	Arlington	VA	33112
9	Honolulu	HA	87590
10	Miami	FL	44512
11	Detroit	MI	77884
12	Seattle	WA	88665
13	Dallas	TX	44556
14			
15	**CITY**	**STATE**	**ZIP**
16			
17			
18	**CITY**	**STATE**	**ZIP**
19	Miami	FL	44512
20	Detroit	MI	77884

A18 and choose "Paste" again. The headings should be duplicated twice as in the illustrated example.

We will now define the database. Select your entire list (cells A3:G13 in the example) and choose "Set Database" from the "Data" menu. Now select the headings at the bottom (A18:G18 in the example) and choose "Define Name" from the "Formula" menu. Name this range of cells "Ext," for "extract."

Using Database

What can "Database" do that "Sort" in the "MAILING_LIST" example couldn't? Let's start with a simple instance. Suppose we are looking for all the names on the list that begin with the letter S. Using "Sort," we could alphabetize the whole list, scroll through until we find the S's, define the records, copy them, and paste them somewhere else. That's the hard way.

The easy way is with a database criteria function. Under the heading "LAST" in cell A16 we will type the letter S. This tells Excel to find all records with a last name beginning with S. (If we typed "Sm" in this cell, Excel would find all records beginning with Sm, such as Smith and Smedley.) We must define the criteria range before the sort and extraction can take place. In other words, we must tell Excel that we are concerned only with last names and only with the letter *S*. To do this, we select cells A15 and A16 and choose "Set Criteria" from the "Data" menu. Now Excel knows exactly what the criteria consist of.

Next, we must tell Excel where to place the extracted records. From the "Formula" menu, select "Goto" and double-click "Ext," which is what we defined the bottom headings as. Now we are ready for the search and extraction to commence. Select "Extract" from the "Data" menu. If there are duplicate records in your list, you might want to check "Unique Records Only" to avoid the duplicates. Click OK. Under the headings, beginning in row 19 (in the example), all records beginning with the letter *S* will be listed.

Let's try a more complicated search. We want to find all records with last names that begin with a letter higher than the letter *E*. Of those, we want only the records with first names that begin with Jo. In cell A16 under "LAST" we enter ">F," meaning higher than F. All comparison operators can be used in this context: (=, >, <, <=, >=, and <>). But why did we choose F when we wanted higher than E? Because Excel is very literal-minded—it considers Fa higher than F. We could have said ">Ez," but we are assuming that there are no last names that consist simply of F. Now in cell B16 we enter "Jo," indicating that a match consists of any first name beginning with Jo, such as John or Joseph.

Now we redefine the criteria area, which consists of A18:B19. Choose "Set Criteria" from the "Data" menu. Next, we tell Excel where to place the extracted names by choosing "Goto" from the "Formula" menu and selecting "Ext." Finally, we select "Extract" from the "Data" menu. The records meeting the new criteria will list below the headings.

A few details. The criteria area must be a continuous selection, meaning that if you want to specify a last name and a zip code, you must put these two headings next to each other and select them together. You're even allowed to use the same heading twice for two criteria in the same field. You don't have to list the field headings in the extracted section in the same order as they are listed in the database, and you don't have to include all of them. You can repeat them more than once. The records will appear in the format in which you have arranged the headings.

Obviously, we have only scratched the surface of what the database search function can do. You could, for example, find records of people within a certain area who spent over a given amount with your company, provided you include sales figures in the database. You could even concoct complex formulas as criteria, such as sorting only records where the quantity of items times the price of items is over a certain amount. In addition to finding and extracting records matching the criteria, you can delete records matching the criteria.

CHAPTER 11

Real Estate Applications

There are a great many real estate applications that can be performed with Excel. Mailing lists can be used to send follow-up letters to clients (see the previous chapter); the productivity of salespeople can be tracked (see Chapter 8); a model constructed to trace cashflow (see Chapter 8) could handle some property management needs; and depreciation can be calculated (see the next chapter).

In this chapter, however, we're going to examine four applications that relate directly to real estate investing:

Finding Present Value
Finding Future Value
Finding the Interest Rate
Amortizing a Loan

FINDING PRESENT VALUE

Purpose

Enter the annual interest rate, the term of the loan, the payment per period, and the future value, and the worksheet shown in Figure 11–1 will compute the present value (or the outstanding principal of the loan). This could be useful if, for example, a mortgage buyer wanted to know how much it would cost to pay off a mortgage early. (Obviously, this worksheet only figures outstanding principal and does not take into account penalties or the extra costs of prepaying a mortgage.)

FIGURE 11-1 Present Value Worksheet

	A	B	C	D
1	(Boldface=User Entry)			
2	Interest Rate (annual)	12.00%	Interest Rate (monthly)	1.00%
3	Term of Loan (months)	360		
4	Monthly Payment	$900.00		
5	Future Value	$100,000.00		
6				
7	Present Value	$90,278.17	total amount owed	$424,000.00
8				
9	payment *	1	number of payments remaining	359
10	total paid to date	$900.00	total of remaining payments	$423,100.00
11				
12	principal remaining	$90,280.95	interest remaining	$332,819.05
13	principal paid to date	($2.78)	interest paid to date	$902.78
14	principal this payment	($2.78)	interest this payment	$902.78

The worksheet also computes the status of the loan after a given number of payments.

Constructing the Model

Set the column widths as follows: A=19, B=11, C=22, and D=11. Type in the labels as illustrated in cell ranges A1:A14 and C2:C14. Select cells B2 and D2 and format them as percentages by choosing "Numbers" from the "Format" menu. Select cells B4, B5, B7, B10, B12:B14, D7, D10, and D12:D14 and format these as dollars and cents by choosing "Number" from the "Format" menu. (The multiple selection of cells can be accomplished through the use of the Command key.) Select cells A1:A5 and A9 and format them as Bold by choosing "Style" from the "Format" menu.

Enter the formulas in their appropriate cells as illustrated (see Figure 11-2).

Using the Present Value Worksheet

Type in the information that goes in cells B2:B5—that is, the annual interest rate, the term (or length) of the loan in months, the monthly payment, and the future value. The present value will be calculated and displayed in cell A7. A monthly payment period is used in this example—if you wish to use a different payment pe-

FIGURE 11-2 Present Value Formulas Worksheet

	A	B	C	D
1				
2	Interest Rate (annual)		Interest Rate (monthly)	=B2/12
3	Term of Loan (months)			
4	Monthly Payment			
5	Future Value			
6				
7	Present Value	=PV(D2,B3,-B4,-B5)	total amount owed	=(B4*B3)+B5
8				
9	payment #		number of payments remaining	=B3-B9
10	total paid to date	=B9*B4	total of remaining payments	=D7-B10
11				
12	principal remaining	=PV(D2,D9,-B4,-B5)	interest remaining	=D10-B12
13	principal paid to date	=B7-B12	interest paid to date	=B10-B13
14	principal this payment	=PV(D2,D9+1,-B4,-B5)-B12	interest this payment	

riod, only the formula in cell D2 need be changed. The formula now takes the entered annual interest rate from cell B2 and divides by 12 to find the monthly interest rate. If, for example, you wished to change the payment period from months to years, you would only need to change the formula in cell D2 to "=B2" so that cell D2 reflects the annual interest rate. You might also wish to change the labels in cells C2, A3, and A4 to avoid confusion, although these have no effect on the amounts computed.

The data in cells A9:D14 are meant to show the status of the loan after a given number of payments. That number can be entered in cell B9. A complete chart of this information can be created by adding the formulas and following the instructions from the "LOAN_AMORTIZATION" worksheet, columns F:I. The chart transposes perfectly into this worksheet.

FINDING FUTURE VALUE

Purpose

Enter the interest rate, the amount of the loan, the term of the loan, and the payment per period, and the worksheet shown in Figure 11-3 will compute the future value. A mortgage buyer might apply future value to determine how much a balloon payment will be after the term of the mortgage has expired. Or an investor might apply it to determine how much a piece of property

FIGURE 11-3 Future Value Worksheet

	A	B	C	D
1	(Boldface=User Entry)			
2	Interest Rate (annual)	12.00%	Interest Rate (monthly)	1.00%
3	Amount of Loan	$100,000.00		
4	Term of Loan (months)	360		
5	Monthly Payment	$900.00		
6				
7	Future Value	$449,496.41	total amount owed	$773,496.41
8				
9	payment #	27	number of payments remaining	333
10	total paid to date	$24,300.00	total of remaining payments	$749,196.41
11				
12	principal remaining	$103,082.09	interest remaining	$646,114.32
13	principal paid to date	($3,082.09)	interest paid to date	$27,382.09
14	principal this payment	($129.53)	interest this payment	$1,029.53

will be worth at a given time in the future if he receives X amount of rent and earns Y amount of interest.

The worksheet also computes the status of the loan after a given number of payments.

Constructing the Model

Set the column widths as follows: A=19, B=11, C=22, and D=11. Type in the labels as illustrated in cell ranges A1:A14 and C2:C14. Select cells B2 and D2 and format them as percentages by choosing "Numbers" from the "Format" menu. Select cells B3, B5, B7, B10, B12:B14, D7, D10, and D12:D14 and format these as dollars and cents by choosing "Number" from the "Format" menu. (The multiple selection of cells can be accomplished through the use of the Command key.) Select cells A1:A5 and A9 and format them as Bold by choosing "Style" from the "Format" menu.

Enter the formulas in their appropriate cells as illustrated (see Figure 11–4).

Using the Future Value Worksheet

Type in the information that goes in cells B2:B5—that is, the annual interest rate, the amount of the loan, the term (or length) of the loan in months, and the monthly payment. The future value will be computed and displayed in cell B7. A monthly payment pe-

FIGURE 11–4   Future Value Formulas Worksheet

	A	B	C	D
1				
2	Interest Rate (annual)	=0.12	Interest Rate (monthly)	=B2/12
3	Amount of Loan			
4	Term of Loan (months)	.		
5	Monthly Payment			
6				
7	Future Value	=FV(D2,B4,B5,-B3)	total amount owed	=(B5*B4)+B7
8				
9	payment #		number of payments remaining	=B4-B9
10	total paid to date	=B9*B5	total of remaining payments	=D7-B10
11				
12	principal remaining	=PV(D2,D9,-B5,-B7)	interest remaining	=D10-B12
13	principal paid to date	=B3-B12	interest paid to date	=B10-B13
14	principal this payment	=PV(D2,D9+1,-B5,-B7)-B12	interest this payment	=B5-B14

riod is used in this example—if you wish to use a different payment period, only the formula in cell D2 need be changed. The formula now takes the entered annual interest rate from cell B2 and divides by 12 to find the monthly interest rate. If, for example, you wished to change the payment period from months to years, you would only need to change the formula in cell D2 to "=B2" so that cell D2 reflects the annual interest rate. You might also wish to change the labels in cells C2, A3, and A4 to avoid confusion, although these have no effect on the amounts computed.

The data in cells A9:D14 are meant to show the status of the loan after a given number of payments. That number can be entered in cell B9. A complete chart of this information can be created by adding the formulas and following the instructions from the "LOAN_AMORTIZATION" worksheet, columns F:I. The chart transposes perfectly into this worksheet.

FINDING THE INTEREST RATE

Purpose

Enter the amount of the loan, the term of the loan, the payment per period, and the future value, and the worksheet shown in Figure 11–5 will compute the interest rate. The worksheet also computes the status of the loan after a given number of payments.

FIGURE 11–5   Interest Rate Worksheet

	A	B	C	D
1	(Boldface=User Entry)			
2	Amount of Loan	$100,000.00	Interest Rate (monthly)	0.90%
3	Term of Loan (months)	360		
4	Monthly Payment	$900.00		
5	Future Value	$100,000.00		
6				
7	Interest Rate (annual)	10.80%	total amount owed	$424,000.00
8				
9	payment #	24	number of payments remaining	336
10	total paid to date	$21,600.00	total of remaining payments	$402,400.00
11				
12	principal remaining	$100,000.00	interest remaining	$302,400.00
13	principal paid to date	$0.00	interest paid to date	$21,600.00
14	principal this payment	$0.00	interest this payment	$900.00

Constructing the Model

Set the column widths as follows: A=19, B=11, C=22, and D=11. Type in the labels as illustrated in cell ranges A1:A14 and C2:C14. Select cells B7 and D2 and format them as percentages by choosing "Numbers" from the "Format" menu. Select cells B2, B4, B5, B10, B12:B14, D7, D10, and D12:D14 and format these as dollars and cents by choosing "Number" from the "Format" menu. (The multiple selection of cells can be accomplished through the use of the Command key.) Select cells A1:A5 and A9 and format them as Bold by choosing "Style" from the "Format" menu.

Enter the formulas in their appropriate cells as illustrated (see Figures 11–6 and 11–7).

Using the Interest Rate Worksheet

Type in the information that goes in cells B2:B5 — that is, the amount of the loan, the term (or length) of the loan in months, the monthly payment and the future value. The monthly interest rate will be computed and displayed in cell D2. The annual interest rate is computed (monthly times 12) and displayed in cell B7. A monthly payment period is used in this example — if you wish to use a different payment period, only the formula in cell B7 need be changed. The formula now takes the computed interest rate from cell D2

FIGURE 11–6   Interest Rate Formulas Worksheet 1

	A	B	C
1	(Boldface=User Entry)		
2	Amount of Loan		Interest Rate (monthly)
3	Term of Loan (months)		
4	Monthly Payment		
5	Future Value		
6			
7	Interest Rate (annual)	=D2*12	total amount owed
8			
9	payment #		number of payments remaining
10	total paid to date	=B9*B4	total of remaining payments
11			
12	principal remaining	=PV(D2,D9,-B4,-B5)	interest remaining
13	principal paid to date	=B2-B12	interest paid to date
14	principal this payment	=PV(D2,D9+1,-B4,-B5)-B12	interest this payment

FIGURE 11–7   Interest Rate Formulas Worksheet 2

	D
1	
2	=RATE(B3,-B4,B2,-B5,0,0.05)
3	
4	
5	
6	
7	=(B4*B3)+B5
8	
9	=B3-B9
10	=D7-B10
11	
12	=D10-B12
13	=B10-B13
14	=B4-B14

and multiplies by 12 to find the annual interest rate. If, for example, you wished to change the payment period from months to years, you would only need to change the formula in cell B7 to "=D2" so that cell B7 reflects the annual interest rate. You might also wish to change the labels in cells C2, A3, and A4 to avoid confusion, although these have no effect on the amounts computed.

In certain cases the interest rate cell and other cells may display "#NUM!" instead of a value. This happens because the guess—the last number in the formula for cell D2—is too far from the actual interest rate. In the illustrated example the guess is 5 percent. If you are getting "#NUM!" try a different value in this formula. Usually a number between 1 percent and 100 percent will provide results, but it may take several tries before a successful computation is made. When in doubt, it is better to guess too high than too low.

The data in cells A9:D14 are meant to show the status of the loan after a given number of payments. That number can be entered in cell B9. A complete chart of this information can be created by adding the formulas and following the instructions from the "LOAN_AMORTIZATION" worksheet, columns F:I. The chart transposes perfectly into this worksheet.

AMORTIZING A LOAN

Purpose

Enter the basic information about the loan (the interest rate, the amount of the loan, the term of the loan) and find out how much the payments come to, how much of a given payment is principal, how much is interest, and how much principal remains after a given payment. The worksheet shown in Figures 11–8, 11–9, and 11–10 also computes the total amount owed and the total amount of interest paid over the life of the loan.

Constructing the Model

Set the column widths as follows: A=19, B=11, C=22, D=11, E=10, F=9, G=17, H=19, and I=18. Type in the labels as illustrated in cell ranges A1:A14 and C2:C14. Note that the labels in cells F2:I2 are merely references to other cells and need not be typed in. Select cells B2 and D2 and format them as percentages by choosing "Numbers" from the "Format" menu. Select cells B3, B7, B10, B12:B14, D7, D10, D12:D14, and G3:I364 and format these as dollars and cents. (The multiple selection can be accomplished through the use of the Command key and, in the case of G3:I364,

FIGURE 11–8 Loan Amortization Worksheet 1

	A	B	C	D
2	**Interest Rate (annual)**	12.00%	Interest Rate (monthly)	1.00%
3	**Amount of Loan**	$100,000.00		
4	**Term of Loan (months)**	360		
5				
6				
7	Monthly Payment	$1,028.61	total amount owed	$370,300.53
8				
9	**payment #**	5	number of payments remaining	355
10	total paid to date	$5,143.06	total of remaining payments	$365,157.47
11				
12	principal remaining	$99,854.05	interest remaining	$265,303.42
13	principal paid to date	$145.95	interest paid to date	$4,997.11
14	principal this payment	$29.77	interest this payment	$998.84

FIGURE 11–9 Loan Amortization Worksheet 2

	F	G	H	I
2	**payment #**	**principal remaining**	**principal this payment**	**interest this payment**
3	5	$99,854.05	$29.77	$998.84
4	0	$100,000.00	$28.33	$1,000.28
5	1	$99,971.39	$28.61	$1,000.00
6	2	$99,942.49	$28.90	$999.71
7	3	$99,913.30	$29.19	$999.42
8	4	$99,883.82	$29.48	$999.13
9	5	$99,854.05	$29.77	$998.84
10	6	$99,823.97	$30.07	$998.54
11	7	$99,793.60	$30.37	$998.24
12	8	$99,762.93	$30.68	$997.94
13	9	$99,731.94	$30.98	$997.63
14	10	$99,700.65	$31.29	$997.32
15	11	$99,669.04	$31.61	$997.01

the Shift key.) Select cells A1:A4, A9, and F2:I2 and format them as Bold by choosing "Style" from the "Format" menu.

Enter the formulas in their appropriate cells as illustrated (see Figures 11–11 and 11–12). You may notice that there are no formulas where the large chart goes; this is because we will use the "Table" command to create it.

FIGURE 11–10 Loan Amortization Worksheet 3

	F	G	H	I
359	355	$4,992.30	$969.00	$59.61
360	356	$4,013.61	$978.69	$49.92
361	357	$3,025.13	$988.48	$40.14
362	358	$2,026.77	$998.36	$30.25
363	359	$1,018.43	$1,008.34	$20.27
364	360	$0.00	$1,018.43	$10.18

FIGURE 11–11 Loan Amortization Formulas 1

	A	B	C	D	E	F	G	H
1								
2	Interest Rate (annual)		Interest Rate (monthly)	=B2/12		=A9	=A12	=A14
3	Amount of Loan						=B12	=B14
4	Term of Loan (months)							
5								
6								
7	Monthly Payment	=PMT(D2,B4,-B3)	total amount owed	=B7*B4				
8								
9	payment #		number of payments remaining	=B4-B9				
10	total paid to date	=B9*B7	total of remaining payments	=D7-B10				
11								
12	principal remaining	=PV(D2,D9,-B7)	interest remaining	=D10-B12				
13	principal paid to date	=B3-B12	interest paid to date	=B10-B13				
14	principal this payment	=PV(D2,D9+1,-B7)-B12	interest this payment	=B7-B14				

FIGURE 11–12 Loan Amortization Formulas 2

	I
1	
2	=C14
3	=D14
4	
5	
6	
7	
8	
9	
10	
11	
12	
13	
14	

Using the Loan Amortization Worksheet

Type in the information that goes in cells B2:B4—that is, the annual interest rate, the amount of the loan, and the term (or length) of the loan in months. A monthly payment period is used in this example—if the period is different, only the formula in cell D2 need be changed. The formula now takes the entered annual interest rate from cell B2 and divides by 12 to find the monthly interest rate. If, for example, you wished to change the payment period from months to years, you would only need to change the formula in cell D2 to "=B2" so that cell D2 reflects the annual interest rate. You might also wish to change the labels in cells C2 and A4 to avoid confusion, although these have no effect on the amounts computed.

The data in cells A9:D14 are meant to show the status of the loan after a given number of payments. That number can be entered in cell B9.

To create a table of the complete loan, we scroll horizontally to view columns F through I. Cells F2:I3 should already be filled in as per their formulas. Select cell F4 and go to the "Series" selection on the "Data" menu. Under "Series in" select "Columns." "Type" should already be "Linear," and "Step Value" should already be "1." If not, type these in. Click the cursor in the "Step Value" box and enter the number of periods in your loan (there are 360 in the illustrated example). Click OK. Column F should fill up with the series of numbers you requested. This could take awhile—particularly in the case of 360—so wait until the cursor is no longer a clock before continuing.

Now select cell range F3:I364 if you've chosen 360 periods, or column I and whatever row your numbers extend down to if you've chosen something different. From the "Data" menu, select "Table." You will be asked to type in an input cell reference in either the "Row" or "Column" box. Type "B9" in the "Column" box to indicate that the numbers in column F will replace the input value in cell B9. You will then see your table fill in slowly. Again, if you have 360 rows to fill in, this could take awhile. Your cursor will appear like a clock until it has been done.

Finally, you may wish to enter the formula "=B9" in cell F3 to indicate what payment number row 3 is referring to. This was left until last because that value would have confused the program when the table was being created.

CHAPTER 12

Investment Applications

Excel is useful for more than just formal business applications. It can also come in handy when you are working with your own investments. In this chapter we'll cover three separate investment models:

Tracking a Stock Portfolio
Calculating Moving Averages
Determining Depreciation

TRACKING A STOCK PORTFOLIO

Purpose

To track a stock portfolio, current market values are calculated and totaled along with gain or loss, estimated annual income, yield, and whether the stock has been held over six months (see Figure 12–1).

Constructing the Model

Set the column widths as follows: A=10, B=11.5, C=11.7, D=10, E=10, F=9, and G=11. Type in the headings in cells A3:F4 and A19:G20 as illustrated. Center-align and boldface them with selections from the "Format" menu. Type in the heading in A30 boldface and right-align it. Clear the gridlines by choosing "Display" from the "Options" menu, and fill in the borders as illustrated by choosing "Border" from the "Format" menu.

FIGURE 12–1   Stock Portfolio Worksheet

	A	B	C	D	E	F	G
1							
2			INPUT				
3	Name	# of	Date	Cost per	Current	Quarterly	
4		Shares	Purchased	Share	Price	Div/Share	
5	BIG CORP.	200	12/22/84	$135.00	$155.50	$0.12	
6	INTL. GLOBAL	300	6/7/85	$50.00	$48.50	$0.05	
7	TRANS FIDEL.	150	8/8/83	$23.50	$33.75	$0.00	
8	MTV	400	6/3/85	$15.00	$22.50	$0.02	
9	MERRILL	175	2/3/85	$25.00	$27.50	$0.23	
10	WORLD ENT.	125	9/22/85	$125.00	$117.00	$1.00	
11	SPACE LINK	250	10/21/84	$5.25	$25.25	$0.00	
12	QUANTITY CO.	50	12/8/84	$12.50	$13.50	$0.10	
13	NEWPORT INC.	500	6/6/85	$5.00	$4.50	$0.00	
14	MICRO COMP.	750	3/4/83	$2.50	$10.25	$0.08	
15	TREETOP	300	10/4/85	$120.00	$115.00	$2.50	
16							
17							
18			OUTPUT				
19	Name	Purchase	Current	Gain	Held Over	Estimated	
20		Price	Value	(Loss)	Six Months	Ann. Income	Yield
21	BIG CORP.	$27,000.00	$31,100.00	$4,100.00	X	$96.00	0.36%
22	INTL. GLOBAL	$15,000.00	$14,550.00	($450.00)	X	$60.00	0.40%
23	TRANS FIDEL.	$3,525.00	$5,062.50	$1,537.50	X	$0.00	
24	MTV	$6,000.00	$9,000.00	$3,000.00	X	$32.00	0.53%
25	MERRILL	$4,375.00	$4,812.50	$437.50	X	$161.00	3.68%
26	WORLD ENT.	$15,625.00	$14,625.00	($1,000.00)		$500.00	3.20%
27	SPACE LINK	$1,312.50	$6,312.50	$5,000.00	X	$0.00	
28	QUANTITY CO.	$625.00	$675.00	$50.00	X	$20.00	3.20%
29	NEWPORT INC.	$2,500.00	$2,250.00	($250.00)	X	$0.00	
30	MICRO COMP.	$1,875.00	$7,687.50	$5,812.50	X	$240.00	12.80%
31	TREETOP	$36,000.00	$34,500.00	($1,500.00)		$3,000.00	8.33%
32							
33	Totals:	$113,837.50	$130,575.00	$16,737.50		$4,109.00	

Enter the formulas as per the illustration (see Figures 12–2 and 12–3). Only some formulas need be typed in—the rest can be filled. Type in cells A21:G21. Then select A21:G21 and choose "Fill Down" from the "Edit" menu. Finally, enter the formulas into B33:D33 and also F33. This completes construction of the model.

Using the Stock Portfolio Model

Only columns A through F need be filled in. The rest is calculated by the worksheet. The worksheet is easily expandable if more stocks need to be added. Simply extend the formulas that were filled and adjust the "SUM" formulas to reflect the new range.

FIGURE 12–2 Stock Portfolio Formulas 1

	A	B	C	D
1				
2		INPUT		
3	Name	# of	Date	Cost per
4		Shares	Purchased	Share
5				
6				
7				
8				
9				
10				
11				
12				
13				
14				
15				
16				
17				
18		OUTPUT		
19	Name	Purchase	Current	Gain
20		Price	Value	(Loss)
21	=A5	=B5*D5	=B5*E5	=(E5-D5)*B5
22	=A6	=B6*D6	=B6*E6	=(E6-D6)*B6
23	=A7	=B7*D7	=B7*E7	=(E7-D7)*B7
24	=A8	=B8*D8	=B8*E8	=(E8-D8)*B8
25	=A9	=B9*D9	=B9*E9	=(E9-D9)*B9
26	=A10	=B10*D10	=B10*E10	=(E10-D10)*B10
27	=A11	=B11*D11	=B11*E11	=(E11-D11)*B11
28	=A12	=B12*D12	=B12*E12	=(E12-D12)*B12
29	=A13	=B13*D13	=B13*E13	=(E13-D13)*B13
30	=A14	=B14*D14	=B14*E14	=(E14-D14)*B14
31	=A15	=B15*D15	=B15*E15	=(E15-D15)*B15
32				
33	Totals:	=SUM(B21:B31)	=SUM(C21:C31)	=SUM(D21:D31)

CALCULATING MOVING AVERAGES

Purpose

Enter sales figures or any set of figures that are constant with regard to period intervals (in the example sales figures over 24 months are used). The worksheet shown in Figure 12–4 will track the moving averages, showing short-term and long-term trends and thus allowing predictions to be made.

FIGURE 12–3 Stock Portfolio Formulas 2

	E	F	G
1			
2			
3	Current	Quarterly	
4	Price	Div/Share	
5			
6			
7			
8			
9			
10			
11			
12			
13			
14			
15			
16			
17			
18			
19	Held Over	Estimated	
20	Six Months	Ann. Income	Yield
21	=IF(C5="","",IF((NOW()-C5)>182,"X",""))	=4*F5*B5	=IF(F21=0,"",F21/B21)
22	=IF(C6="","",IF((NOW()-C6)>182,"X",""))	=4*F6*B6	=IF(F22=0,"",F22/B22)
23	=IF(C7="","",IF((NOW()-C7)>182,"X",""))	=4*F7*B7	=IF(F23=0,"",F23/B23)
24	=IF(C8="","",IF((NOW()-C8)>182,"X",""))	=4*F8*B8	=IF(F24=0,"",F24/B24)
25	=IF(C9="","",IF((NOW()-C9)>182,"X",""))	=4*F9*B9	=IF(F25=0,"",F25/B25)
26	=IF(C10="","",IF((NOW()-C10)>182,"X",""))	=4*F10*B10	=IF(F26=0,"",F26/B26)
27	=IF(C11="","",IF((NOW()-C11)>182,"X",""))	=4*F11*B11	=IF(F27=0,"",F27/B27)
28	=IF(C12="","",IF((NOW()-C12)>182,"X",""))	=4*F12*B12	=IF(F28=0,"",F28/B28)
29	=IF(C13="","",IF((NOW()-C13)>182,"X",""))	=4*F13*B13	=IF(F29=0,"",F29/B29)
30	=IF(C14="","",IF((NOW()-C14)>182,"X",""))	=4*F14*B14	=IF(F30=0,"",F30/B30)
31	=IF(C15="","",IF((NOW()-C15)>182,"X",""))	=4*F15*B15	=IF(F31=0,"",F31/B31)
32			
33		=SUM(F21:F31)	
34			
35			
36			
37			

Constructing the Model

Set the column widths as follows: A=6, B=9, C=10, D=12, E=12, and F=13. Remove the gridlines by choosing "Display" from the "Options" menu. Replace the borders as per the illustration by choosing "Border" from the "Format" menu. Type in the labels in

FIGURE 12–4 Moving Average Worksheet

	A	B	C	D	E	F
1	Months	Sales	Trend	3 Month Aver.	6 Month Aver.	12 Month Aver.
2						
3	1	$1,200.00	$1,449.32			
4	2	$1,135.00	$1,486.32			
5	3	$1,365.00	$1,523.33	$1,233.33		
6	4	$2,478.00	$1,560.33	$1,659.33		
7	5	$1,340.00	$1,597.34	$1,727.67		
8	6	$1,280.00	$1,634.34	$1,699.33	$1,466.33	
9	7	$1,567.00	$1,671.35	$1,395.67	$1,527.50	
10	8	$2,090.00	$1,708.35	$1,645.67	$1,686.67	
11	9	$1,765.00	$1,745.36	$1,807.33	$1,753.33	
12	10	$1,190.00	$1,782.36	$1,681.67	$1,538.67	
13	11	$1,679.00	$1,819.37	$1,544.67	$1,595.17	
14	12	$1,390.00	$1,856.37	$1,419.67	$1,613.50	$1,539.92
15	13	$2,970.00	$1,893.38	$2,013.00	$1,847.33	$1,687.42
16	14	$2,100.00	$1,930.38	$2,153.33	$1,849.00	$1,767.83
17	15	$2,400.00	$1,967.39	$2,490.00	$1,954.83	$1,854.08
18	16	$1,780.00	$2,004.39	$2,093.33	$2,053.17	$1,795.92
19	17	$1,900.00	$2,041.40	$2,026.67	$2,090.00	$1,842.58
20	18	$3,500.00	$2,078.40	$2,393.33	$2,441.67	$2,027.58
21	19	$2,280.00	$2,115.41	$2,560.00	$2,326.67	$2,087.00
22	20	$1,670.00	$2,152.41	$2,483.33	$2,255.00	$2,052.00
23	21	$1,878.00	$2,189.42	$1,942.67	$2,168.00	$2,061.42
24	22	$2,200.00	$2,226.42	$1,916.00	$2,238.00	$2,145.58
25	23	$1,970.00	$2,263.43	$2,016.00	$2,249.67	$2,169.83
26	24	$1,870.00	$2,300.43	$2,013.33	$1,978.00	$2,209.83

cells A1:F1, and boldface and center-align them by choosing "Style" and "Alignment" from the "Format" menu. Select columns B through F and format them for dollars and cents by choosing "Number" from the "Format" menu.

Most of the formulas shown in Figures 12–5 and 12–6 can be "filled." In fact, only five formulas need be typed in by hand: in cells A4, D5, E8, F14, and C3. Hold up on cell C3 for now and fill in the other four cells as follows: Type the formula in the cell as per the illustration; select the cell just entered and drag the selection down to row 26 of the same column; and choose "Fill Down" from the "Edit" menu.

Cell C3 is filled in a little differently from the others. Select C3:C26 and type the formula into C3. Hold down the Command key before pressing "Enter." In this way an array is being defined.

FIGURE 12–5 Moving Average Formulas 1

	A	B	C	D	E
1	Months	Sales	Trend	3 Month Aver.	6 Month Aver.
2					
3	1		=TREND(B3:B26)		
4	=1+A3		=TREND(B3:B26)		
5	=1+A4		=TREND(B3:B26)	=(B5+B4+B3)/3	
6	=1+A5		=TREND(B3:B26)	=(B6+B5+B4)/3	
7	=1+A6		=TREND(B3:B26)	=(B7+B6+B5)/3	
8	=1+A7		=TREND(B3:B26)	=(B8+B7+B6)/3	=(B8+B7+B6+B5+B4+B3)/6
9	=1+A8		=TREND(B3:B26)	=(B9+B8+B7)/3	=(B9+B8+B7+B6+B5+B4)/6
10	=1+A9		=TREND(B3:B26)	=(B10+B9+B8)/3	=(B10+B9+B8+B7+B6+B5)/6
11	=1+A10		=TREND(B3:B26)	=(B11+B10+B9)/3	=(B11+B10+B9+B8+B7+B6)/6
12	=1+A11		=TREND(B3:B26)	=(B12+B11+B10)/3	=(B12+B11+B10+B9+B8+B7)/6
13	=1+A12		=TREND(B3:B26)	=(B13+B12+B11)/3	=(B13+B12+B11+B10+B9+B8)/6
14	=1+A13		=TREND(B3:B26)	=(B14+B13+B12)/3	=(B14+B13+B12+B11+B10+B9)/6
15	=1+A14		=TREND(B3:B26)	=(B15+B14+B13)/3	=(B15+B14+B13+B12+B11+B10)/6
16	=1+A15		=TREND(B3:B26)	=(B16+B15+B14)/3	=(B16+B15+B14+B13+B12+B11)/6
17	=1+A16		=TREND(B3:B26)	=(B17+B16+B15)/3	=(B17+B16+B15+B14+B13+B12)/6
18	=1+A17		=TREND(B3:B26)	=(B18+B17+B16)/3	=(B18+B17+B16+B15+B14+B13)/6
19	=1+A18		=TREND(B3:B26)	=(B19+B18+B17)/3	=(B19+B18+B17+B16+B15+B14)/6
20	=1+A19		=TREND(B3:B26)	=(B20+B19+B18)/3	=(B20+B19+B18+B17+B16+B15)/6
21	=1+A20		=TREND(B3:B26)	=(B21+B20+B19)/3	=(B21+B20+B19+B18+B17+B16)/6
22	=1+A21		=TREND(B3:B26)	=(B22+B21+B20)/3	=(B22+B21+B20+B19+B18+B17)/6
23	=1+A22		=TREND(B3:B26)	=(B23+B22+B21)/3	=(B23+B22+B21+B20+B19+B18)/6
24	=1+A23		=TREND(B3:B26)	=(B24+B23+B22)/3	=(B24+B23+B22+B21+B20+B19)/6
25	=1+A24		=TREND(B3:B26)	=(B25+B24+B23)/3	=(B25+B24+B23+B22+B21+B20)/6
26	=1+A25		=TREND(B3:B26)	=(B26+B25+B24)/3	=(B26+B25+B24+B23+B22+B21)/6

Using the Moving Average Model

Enter figures for the period into cells B3:B26. Columns C through F will fill in, but they will not be entirely accurate until all of column C has been filled in. These numbers show the short- and long-term moving averages—that is, the general trend of the numbers in column B. The three-month average is the shortest term, and the Trend column is the longest term, using linear regression to completely even out the jumps. If a period length other than 24 periods is used, the formulas in columns A, D, E, and F can easily be extended or cut off. The trend formula in column C simply needs to be altered by entering the new range.

The data calculated on this worksheet can be comprehended best when they are seen in chart form. In Chapter 13 this worksheet will be used as an example showing how to create a chart.

FIGURE 12–6 Moving Average Formulas 2

	F
1	12 Month Aver.
2	
3	
4	
5	
6	
7	
8	
9	
10	
11	
12	
13	
14	=SUM(B3:B14)/12
15	=SUM(B4:B15)/12
16	=SUM(B5:B16)/12
17	=SUM(B6:B17)/12
18	=SUM(B7:B18)/12
19	=SUM(B8:B19)/12
20	=SUM(B9:B20)/12
21	=SUM(B10:B21)/12
22	=SUM(B11:B22)/12
23	=SUM(B12:B23)/12
24	=SUM(B13:B24)/12
25	=SUM(B14:B25)/12
26	=SUM(B15:B26)/12

DETERMINING DEPRECIATION

Purpose

The worksheet shown in Figures 12–7 and 12–8 calculates the yearly depreciation allowance on a given asset. It takes into account such variables as the first-year expense allowance, the income tax credit (ITC), whether the asset is real property, and the ACRS life of a personal asset. (*Note:* The method of calculating depreciation on real property for tax purposes changes periodically. In this model, a 20-year life is shown. However, your accountant may prefer to use an ACRS life for real property. If so, that requires a separate table for calculations not indicated here.)

FIGURE 12–7 Depreciation Worksheet 1

	A	B	C	D	E	F
1						
2	Asset:				Camera Equipment	
3	Cost:				$16,700.00	
4						
5	Real Property (straight line)					
6	Life:				8	
7						
8	Personal Property (ACRS)					
9	Life (enter 3 or 5 years):				0	
10	Income Tax Credit (enter %):				0%	
11	Amount Expensed First Year (if any):				$0.00	
12						
13						
14	Period	First Year Expense	ITC	Depreciation Expense	Remaining Basis	
15						
16	1	$0.00	$0	$2,087.50	$14,612.50	
17	2			$2,087.50	$12,525.00	
18	3			$2,087.50	$10,437.50	
19	4			$2,087.50	$8,350.00	
20	5			$2,087.50	$6,262.50	
21	6			$2,087.50	$4,175.00	
22	7			$2,087.50	$2,087.50	
23	8			$2,087.50	$0.00	
24	9			$0.00	$0.00	
25	10			$0.00	$0.00	
26	11			$0.00	$0.00	
27	12			$0.00	$0.00	
28	13			$0.00	$0.00	
29	14			$0.00	$0.00	
30	15			$0.00	$0.00	
31	16			$0.00	$0.00	
32	17			$0.00	$0.00	
33	18			$0.00	$0.00	
34	19			$0.00	$0.00	
35	20			$0.00	$0.00	

Special Note

It must be understood that allowable depreciation life, tax credits, and other items associated with depreciation are subject to change. Before using this worksheet, be sure to check with a competent professional for the current parameters. No assurance or guarantee is given that the results from this worksheet will be acceptable by any taxing authority.

Constructing the Model

Set the column widths as follows: A=6, B=15.5, C=7, D=18, and E=13.5. Columns G and H will also be used, but they can be left

FIGURE 12–8 Depreciation Worksheet 2

	G	H
1		
2		
3		
4		
5		
6	4175	2505
7	6346	3674
8	6179	3507
9		3507
10		3507
11		
12		
13		
14		
15		
16		
17		
18		
19		
20		
21		
22		
23		
24		
25		
26		
27		
28		
29		
30		
31		
32		
33		
34		
35		

at the standard width of 10. Use the "Display" selection on the "Options" menu to remove the gridlines, then replace the borders as illustrated by using "Border" on the "Format" menu. Type in the headings in cells A2:A11 and A14:E14 as illustrated, and boldface them by choosing "Style" on the "Format" menu. Center-align cells A14:E14. Select cells E3, E11, and range B16:E20 (make the multiple selection by use of the Command key) and format these as dollars and cents by choosing "Number" from the "Format" menu. Select cell E10 and format it as a percentage by choosing "Numbers" from the "Format" menu.

Now enter the formulas into their appropriate cells as illustrated (see Figures 12–9, 12–10, and 12–11). Typing can be minimized by "filling" certain columns: Type in A15, select A16:A35, and choose "Fill Down" from the "Edit" menu. Type B16 and C16.

FIGURE 12–9   Depreciation Formulas 1

	A	B	C
1			
2	Asset:		
3	Cost:		
4			
5	Real Property (straight line)		
6	Life:		
7			
8	Personal Property (ACRS)		
9	Life (enter 3 or 5 years):		
10	Income Tax Credit (enter %):		
11	Amount Expensed First Year (if any):		
12			
13			
14	Period	First Year Expense	ITC
15			
16	1	=E11	=E3*E10
17	=1+A16		
18	=1+A17		
19	=1+A18		
20	=1+A19		
21	=1+A20		
22	=1+A21		
23	=1+A22		
24	=1+A23		
25	=1+A24		
26	=1+A25		
27	=1+A26		
28	=1+A27		
29	=1+A28		
30	=1+A29		
31	=1+A30		
32	=1+A31		
33	=1+A32		
34	=1+A33		
35	=1+A34		

FIGURE 12-10 Depreciation Formulas 2

	D	E
1		
2		Camera Equipment
3		
4		
5		
6		
7		
8		
9		
10		
11		
12		
13		
14	Depreciation Expense	Remaining Basis
15		
16	=IF($E$9=3,G6,IF($E$9=5,H6,IF(A16>$E$6,0,($E$3/$E$6))))	=$E$3-D16
17	=IF($E$9=3,G7,IF($E$9=5,H7,IF(A17>$E$6,0,($E$3/$E$6))))	=E16-D17
18	=IF($E$9=3,G8,IF($E$9=5,H8,IF(A18>$E$6,0,($E$3/$E$6))))	=E17-D18
19	=IF($E$9=3,G9,IF($E$9=5,H9,IF(A19>$E$6,0,($E$3/$E$6))))	=E18-D19
20	=IF($E$9=3,G10,IF($E$9=5,H10,IF(A20>$E$6,0,($E$3/$E$6))))	=E19-D20
21	=IF($E$9=3,G11,IF($E$9=5,H11,IF(A21>$E$6,0,($E$3/$E$6))))	=E20-D21
22	=IF($E$9=3,G12,IF($E$9=5,H12,IF(A22>$E$6,0,($E$3/$E$6))))	=E21-D22
23	=IF($E$9=3,G13,IF($E$9=5,H13,IF(A23>$E$6,0,($E$3/$E$6))))	=E22-D23
24	=IF($E$9=3,G14,IF($E$9=5,H14,IF(A24>$E$6,0,($E$3/$E$6))))	=E23-D24
25	=IF($E$9=3,G15,IF($E$9=5,H15,IF(A25>$E$6,0,($E$3/$E$6))))	=E24-D25
26	=IF($E$9=3,G16,IF($E$9=5,H16,IF(A26>$E$6,0,($E$3/$E$6))))	=E25-D26
27	=IF($E$9=3,G17,IF($E$9=5,H17,IF(A27>$E$6,0,($E$3/$E$6))))	=E26-D27
28	=IF($E$9=3,G18,IF($E$9=5,H18,IF(A28>$E$6,0,($E$3/$E$6))))	=E27-D28
29	=IF($E$9=3,G19,IF($E$9=5,H19,IF(A29>$E$6,0,($E$3/$E$6))))	=E28-D29
30	=IF($E$9=3,G20,IF($E$9=5,H20,IF(A30>$E$6,0,($E$3/$E$6))))	=E29-D30
31	=IF($E$9=3,G21,IF($E$9=5,H21,IF(A31>$E$6,0,($E$3/$E$6))))	=E30-D31
32	=IF($E$9=3,G22,IF($E$9=5,H22,IF(A32>$E$6,0,($E$3/$E$6))))	=E31-D32
33	=IF($E$9=3,G23,IF($E$9=5,H23,IF(A33>$E$6,0,($E$3/$E$6))))	=E32-D33
34	=IF($E$9=3,G24,IF($E$9=5,H24,IF(A34>$E$6,0,($E$3/$E$6))))	=E33-D34
35	=IF($E$9=3,G25,IF($E$9=5,H25,IF(A35>$E$6,0,($E$3/$E$6))))	=E34-D35

Type in D16 and fill down through D35. Type in E16 separately. Then fill down E17:E35. Don't forget to type in G6:G8 and H6:H10.

Using the Depreciation Model

Now the hard part is over (constructing the model) and the easy part begins. Simply enter the information asked for in cells E2:E3

FIGURE 12–11 Depreciation Formulas 3

	F	G	H
1			
2			
3			
4			
5			
6		=(E3-B16-C16)*0.25	=(E3-B16-C16)*0.15
7		=(E3-B16-C16)*0.38	=(E3-B16-C16)*0.22
8		=(E3-B16-C16)*0.37	=($E$3-$B$16-$C$16)*0.21
9			=($E$3-$B$16-$C$16)*0.21
10			=($E$3-$B$16-$C$16)*0.21
11			
12			
13			
14			
15			
16			
17			
18			
19			
20			
21			
22			
23			
24			
25			
26			
27			
28			
29			
30			
31			
32			
33			
34			
35			

and then either E6 *or* E9 through E11. Refer to your tax manual if you do not understand some of the entries. Cell C16 contains your first-year tax credit. Cells D16:D35 contain your depreciation deductions for the first and subsequent years.

CHAPTER 13

Application Extras

We've covered conventional applications for Excel in previous chapters. Here we will discuss two applications utilizing features that are, as of this writing, unique to Excel. These applications are:

Creating a Chart
Word Processing

CREATING A CHART

Purpose

A chart graphically illustrating numeric data can be read and comprehended much more quickly than columns of numbers. This section shows how to create such a chart. The moving averages application from Chapter 12 will be used as an example.

Specific Examples

Activate the worksheet from which you wish to derive a chart. In this case we will use Figure 12–4, the "MOVING_AVERAGES" worksheet in Chapter 12. Select the range of cells that will be charted. We have selected B3:C26, or "Sales" and "Trend." We could put the other moving averages on the chart, but this would make it too busy and difficult to read. A better solution would be to create different charts for the other moving averages. We will do this later.

Now select "New" from the "File" menu and specify "Chart." A chart will appear, probably a column chart. In this case we prefer to make a combination chart. From the "Gallery" menu, select "Combination." You will see a variety of charts to choose from— choose the first selection for now. Later you may wish to go back and experiment with other varieties of chart formats.

Now we have a chart that we can save (see Figure 13–1). But maybe we want to chart some of the other moving averages. Let's go back to the worksheet by selecting "MOVING_AVERAGE" from the "Window" menu.

We will now create a chart of the sales versus the 12-month moving average (see Figure 13–2). We must do some rearranging on the worksheet, because in order to chart these two columns they must be next to each other. Select column C and then select "Insert" from the "Edit" menu. Now select column F, in Figure 12–4 which is the 12-month moving average, and transfer it over to empty column C by choosing "Cut" from the "Edit" menu, selecting column C, and then choosing "Paste" from the "Edit" menu. Finally, we select cells B3:C26 and create a new chart from the "File" menu. We already know how to convert this into a combination chart.

FIGURE 13–1   Chart 1

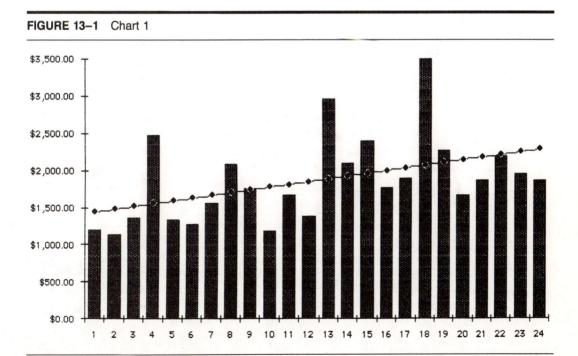

FIGURE 13–2   Chart 2

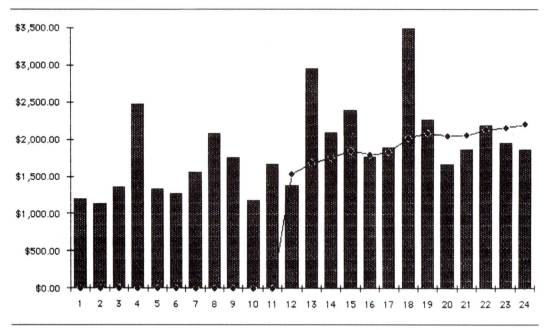

WORD PROCESSING

Purpose

Word processing is not usually the reason a person buys a spread-sheet program such as Excel. Occasionally, however, a spreadsheet user may need to use a word processing application, such as when writing a report that is attached to a worksheet. When that happens, it's nice to know that Excel can accommodate, with just a little bit of cheating.

Constructing the Model

For word processing we need to use Excel in a way that it wasn't really intended to be used. First, we need to increase the width of the A column to fill the screen. The easiest way to do this is to just drag the column divider on the title row over to the far right. (Or we can drag down "Format" to "Column Width" and set it to 63.5.)

Now we have a page on which to write. The next thing we need to do is get rid of all those gridlines, row numbers, and column letters. We do this by dragging down "Options" to "Display." We now click "Gridlines" and "Row & Column" to remove them. When we return to the sheet, we have a clean slate ready for writing.

The outlined cell indicates where our first writing will go. This time, we watch the cell, not the formula bar, as we enter data. When we get to the end of the cell, we hit "Return" just as we would on a typewriter and continue on the next line. Indents can be made by several taps on the space bar.

Editing of our "manuscript" can be accomplished by using the Backspace key while we're typing. Editing of virtually any other kind can be accomplished by highlighting the area in question with the mouse pointer and then rewriting as desired. (*Note: All editing must be done in the formula bar.*)

In this fashion we can get Excel to perform the basic functions of a word processor. A word processing example is shown in Figure 13–3.

Printing Note

When printing out, you may discover that although Excel does not display any gridlines or column or row headings, it prints them on your sheet. To print without these, drag down "File" to "Page

---

FIGURE 13–3 Word Processing Example

Wordprocessing_example

    Yesterday, while strolling down the boulevard, I saw a cat in some
distress. It had apparently been fishing down a barred drainage cover
for some delectable piece of food. Unfortunately, in the process it
managed to get its paw stuck, between the bars. Now it was mewing in the
most pathetic way. What was worse, it was in danger of being hit by any
car driven too close to the gutter.
    I felt called upon to take immediate action. Bending over, I soothed
the worried animal by petting it on the head with one hand while with
my other hand I gently made loose its paw. In a moment it was done.
With what I could only take as a squeal of delight, the cat bounded
free.
    I felt I had done my good deed for that day.

Setup." At the bottom of the box that appears, you will find two headings: "PRINT ROW & COLUMN HEADINGS" and "PRINT GRIDLINES." Excel's default settings include printing these items. Remove the X's by clicking. Excel will now print without gridlines, or row or column headings.

CHAPTER 14

Excel Reference Guide

Although this reference guide includes Excel commands, it is arranged, not by menu, but by use. For example, if you want to set up a chart, go to the "Charting" section. There you will find a series of questions regarding charting, one of which should be similar to yours. Immediately after the question will be the menu reference or the technique required to answer it.

In other words, this reference guide is designed to be a problem solver. If you define your problem before coming to it, you will find that it will quickly and easily give you the answers you need.

CHARTING

How Do I Open a Chart Sheet?

Drag down FILE to NEW. When the dialog box appears, select CHART. Press OK and a chart will appear on-screen.

How Do I Open an Old Chart?

Drag down FILE to OPEN. The list of files on the active diskette will display. Select a chart to open, select a different drive, or eject the current diskette and insert a different one with the correct chart on it.

FIGURE 14–1   Charting

Gallery	Chart	Format
Gallery	**Chart**	**Format**
Area...	Main Chart Type...	Patterns...
Bar...	Overlay Chart Type...	
Column...	Set Preferred Format	Main Chart...
Line...	Axes...	Overlay Chart...
Pie...	Add Legend	Main Chart Axis...
Scatter...	Attach Text...	Legend...
Combination...	Add Arrow	Text...
Preferred	Select Chart	
	Select Plot Area	
	Calculate Now	

How Do I Get the Chart to Refer to Specific Values on My Worksheet?

Before opening the chart, highlight the values you want to refer to. Now open a new chart. It will automatically chart what you have highlighted.

Will the Chart Change if I Change a Value on the Worksheet?

Yes, if the new value is in the range initially highlighted (see above), the chart will automatically recalculate.

How Do I Add New Values (Expand a Range) for a Chart Once the Chart Has Already Been Created?

Adding to a chart requires use of the COPY/PASTE commands. Activate the worksheet and highlight the values you want added to the chart. Drag down EDIT to COPY. The values should now have a floating border around them.

Now activate the existing chart. Drag down EDIT to PASTE or PASTE SPECIAL (see the "Editing" section). The new values will immediately be added to the chart.

How Can I Change the Order of the Plot in a Chart?

You have to change the formula on which the plot is based. Call up the chart and aim the arrow at the plot (the bar, for example, in a bar chart). The data series formula on which the chart is based will appear in the formula bar.

The last two arguments determine the order of the plot. Changing these arguments will change the plot.

How Can I Remove a Bar, Line, Etc. Plot from a Graph?

Aim the pointer at the plot you want removed, then click. A small circle will appear indicating the plot. Now look up at the formula bar. There you will see the data series representing that plot. Simply hit BACKSPACE once (to clear the formula), then ENTER. The formula and its corresponding plot will disappear.

How Do I Create a Legend?

Use the ADD LEGEND command from the CHART menu. (Be sure the names you want identified were included in the range originally identified for the chart. If not, you will have to extend or re-create the appropriate range.)

To delete the legend, you can now use CHART, DELETE LEGEND.

To move the legend to a different spot, use FORMAT, LEGEND.

To change the style of the legend, first select the legend by aiming and clicking at it, then drag down FORMAT to PATTERNS.

How Do I Add Text to a Chart?

Without selecting any part of the chart, simply type what text you want, then ENTER. The text will appear on the chart surrounded by black boxes. Clicking the mouse while aiming away from the boxes will remove them.

You can move this "unattached" text by clicking it. The black boxes will appear. Now drag the box to wherever you want it on the chart.

You can enlarge or decrease the size of the text area by aiming at one of the small black boxes and dragging.

You can change the text by clicking it and then editing in the normal way in the formula box.

You can delete text by selecting it, and then hitting BACKSPACE and ENTER.

You may also "attach" text to various areas of the chart using the CHART, ATTACH TEXT command. Using this command will call up a box that will give a series of obvious choices (the category axis is usually at the bottom, and the value axis is usually along the left side) for placement. The position where material is to go will be highlighted with circles on the chart. Simply type what you want (which will appear in the formula box). When you've finished, hit ENTER and the material will move to the chart.

You can change the background, border pattern, weight, and style of any text by selecting FORMAT, PATTERNS *after* you have *first* selected the text by aiming at it and clicking.

Can I Add an Arrow to a Chart?

Yes, just drag down to ADD ARROW from the CHART menu. Once the arrow has been drawn, you can move it, lengthen it, or shorten it by aiming the pointer at the front or the back, clicking, and dragging to where you want the arrow to go.

The arrow can be darkened, its pattern changed, or its head enlarged by selecting FORMAT, PATTERNS after you have first selected the arrow by aiming at it and clicking.

Can I Change the Axis Formats?

Select by aiming and clicking the particular axis you want changed. Then drag down to PATTERNS from the FORMAT menu and make your selections.

Can I Put Gridlines into My Chart?

Select the AXES command from the CHART menu. You can now select major or minor gridlines for either category or values.

The format of these gridlines can be changed by selecting one line (aiming and clicking), then dragging down to PATTERNS from the FORMAT menu.

How Do I Get a Different Chart Format (Bar, Line, Pie, Etc.)?

To get a different "type" of chart, use MAIN CHART from the CHART menu.

To select a different FORMAT for a given type of chart, use the GALLERY menu. It will display all of the available formats.

(*Note:* Pie charts display only one data series.) The format selected appears in reverse image.

The "preferred format" is Excel's choice for you when you open a chart. It is always a column chart, number 1 from the GALLERY menu. (You can choose a different "preferred format" by selecting SET PREFERRED FORMAT from the CHART menu.)

If you haven't already done so, exploring the different formats available from the GALLERY menu is worth a few moments' time.

Can I Overlay One Chart on Another?

Use the GALLERY COMBINATION command. This will give you four different overlay types that you may use. Once you have created the overlay, you may change it by using OVERLAY TYPE CHART from the CHART menu. A box will appear and give you a variety of choices. To remove the overlay, select NONE; to keep the overlay, select one of the others. Excel will divide the data series and put half on the overlay and half on the main chart.

DATA PROCESSING

There are relatively few data processing commands. See Chapter 5, "Data Processing," for information on how to create a database and on how to define the criteria and extract ranges. The following commands will be useful as a quick reminder of how to operate Excel's data processing features.

FIGURE 14–2   Data Processing

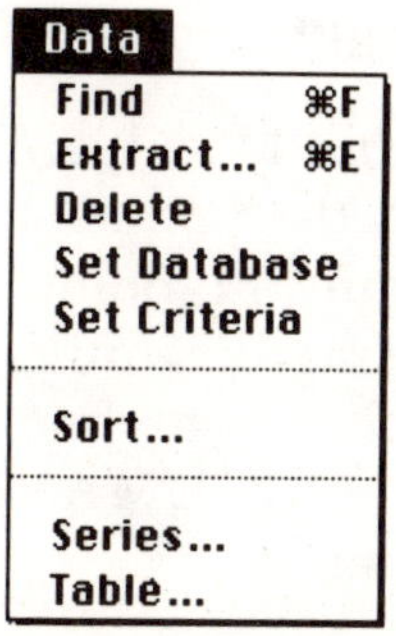

```
Data
Find          ⌘F
Extract...    ⌘E
Delete
Set Database
Set Criteria
..............
Sort...
..............
Series...
Table...
```

How Do I Define a Database for Excel?

To define the database, first outline it, then use the DATA, SET DATABASE command. Nothing visible happens on-screen, but Excel now knows where the database is.

To define the criteria range, use the same procedure but substitute DATA, SET CRITERIA.

How Do I Find Records in the Database?

When the database and criteria (and extract) ranges have been properly defined (see Chapter 5), the DATA, FIND command will locate the records matching the criteria. The DATA, EXTRACT command will locate the records and then send them to a designated location (provided an extract range has been defined).

How Do I Sort?

Use the DATA, SORT command and fill in the required information under one or more of the keys. Sorting is automatic as soon as OK has been selected.

Can I Create a Table Using the Database?

Yes, use DATA, TABLE. You'll need to input both row and column cell locations.

EDITING

How Do I Highlight Material?

With Excel and Mac, highlighting is a breeze. To highlight a single cell, just aim the pointer at it and click the mouse. To highlight a range, just aim the pointer at one corner, hold the mouse button down, and drag diagonally across to the opposite corner. To highlight discontinuously, highlight the first range as indicated above, then press the COMMAND key and highlight the next range and repeat as desired.

FIGURE 14–3   Editing

```
┌─────────────────────────┐
│ Edit                    │
│ Undo            ⌘Z      │
│ Cut             ⌘H      │
│ Copy            ⌘C      │
│ Paste           ⌘U      │
│ Clear...        ⌘B      │
│ Paste Special...        │
│·························  │
│ Delete...       ⌘K      │
│ Insert...       ⌘I      │
│·························  │
│ Fill Right      ⌘R      │
│ Fill Down       ⌘D      │
└─────────────────────────┘
```

How Do I Enter Material?

Data can only be entered into an active cell (see below). Simply type whatever you want to enter. (*Note:* If you want to enter a formula, the first thing to appear must be the equal [=] sign.)

Whatever is typed will appear on the "formula bar"; this is the line just below the menus. You will see it appear both here and in the cell as you type. However, the data is only temporary until it has been entered into a cell. While in the formula bar, the material can be erased or edited.

Once you have the correct information in the formula bar, it can be entered into a cell in two ways. The first way is to tap the ENTER key. The second way is to activate any other cell.

How Do I Activate a New Cell?

There are several ways to do this:

1. Use the mouse to aim at a different cell. Click once and that cell will be activated.
2. Tap the RETURN key. The next cell down will be activated. (*Note:* If the RETURN key is used at the bottom row inside a range, the cell at the top of the next column to the right will be activated.) To activate the cell immediately above the current cell, hold down SHIFT while tapping RETURN. To ac-

tivate the cell to the right of the current cell, use RETURN. To activate the cell to the left of the current cell, use SHIFT, RETURN.

How Do I Edit Data?

To edit data, you must first activate the cell in which they are written. Once the cell has been activated, its contents will appear in the formula bar. They may be edited here.

Use the BACKSPACE to remove material from right to left. Use the mouse to highlight material in the formula bar that you want changed or deleted. Highlighted material will disappear at the next keystroke. To insert material, aim the pointer at the spot of insertion and click once. A cursor will appear, and material may be typed in at that spot from left to right.

To delete *all* the material in a cell while working in the formula bar, hit ENTER first; then, while the cell is active, tap BACKSPACE. Whatever is in the cell will immediately be erased. To leave the cell, now tap ENTER and move to another cell.

How Do I Move Cells (Information) from One Spot to Another?

To move cells, you must use the CUT and PASTE commands.

First, highlight whatever you want moved. Now use EDIT, CUT. In a moment a wavy border will appear around the material to be moved.

Now aim at the spot where the material is to be moved and click once, activating that cell. (If a range is being moved, aim at where you want the upper-left cell of the range to appear.) Now drag down PASTE. The material will disappear from its original position and appear in the new one.

(*Note:* PASTE SPECIAL only works with the COPY command, discussed below.)

How Do I Copy Data?

To copy data, follow the same instructions as those given above for moving. However, instead of using the CUT command (from the EDIT menu), use the COPY command.

When pasting with the COPY command, you have the option of using PASTE SPECIAL. If this command is selected, you will be given a special option box. In it you can choose whether to paste everything in the copied cells or only formulas, values, or formats. In addition, you can choose to have four basic operations (+, −, *, /) performed while the material is being pasted.

How Do I Insert Cells, Rows, or Columns?

Use the EDIT, INSERT command. To insert one or more rows, highlight the row number(s) where you want the new row(s) to appear. Then use EDIT, INSERT. The old rows will shift down, allowing the new row(s) to appear.

To insert one or more columns, highlight the letter(s) above the column(s) where you want the new column(s) to appear. Then use EDIT, INSERT. The old columns will shift right, allowing the new column(s) to appear.

To insert one or more cells, highlight where you want the cell(s) inserted and use EDIT, INSERT. You will be given a choice of whether you want the existing cells shifted right or down to make room for the new cell(s).

How Do I Delete Cells, Rows, or Columns?

Follow the same procedure as that given above, but use EDIT, DELETE. The highlighted cell(s), row(s), or column(s) will be deleted.

Can I Clear Data without Deleting Cells?

Yes, use the EDIT, CLEAR command. You must first, however, highlight whatever you want cleared. Then you will be given a choice of clearing the formats, the formulas, or everything in the highlighted cells.

Can I Undo What I've Just Done?

Yes, most times you can undo your last command. Just use EDIT, UNDO. It will indicate the last command that can be undone.

How Do I Fill in a Range?

First, highlight the range you want filled. Be sure that whatever you want to fill it with is in the top-left cell. Then just use the

EDIT, FILL DOWN or EDIT, FILL RIGHT commands. Whatever was in the top-left cell will be duplicated in all the cells of the range.

(*Note:* This is different from filling in a series, for example, having a row of cells fill with the months of the year. To do that, follow the same procedure as that given above, being sure that what is to be filled follows one of Excel's accepted formats—found in the FORMAT menu. Then, instead of using EDIT, FILL, use DATA, SERIES.)

FILE MANAGEMENT

How Do I Open a File?

When you turn on Excel you will automatically be in a new worksheet. If you want to call up a *new* file, use the command FILE, NEW. Excel will give you the option of opening a worksheet, a macro sheet, or a chart.

If you want to open an existing file, use FILE, OPEN. Excel will display the contents of the active diskette (usually the external drive). You may make a selection, or you can choose DRIVE to select from a diskette in the other drive.

If you have files that are linked to the active document, they can be opened using the FILE, OPEN LINKS command.

FIGURE 14–4 File Management

```
File
New...        ⌘N
Open...       ⌘O
Open Links...
Close All
Save          ⌘S
Save As...
Delete...

Page Setup...
Print...      ⌘P
Printer Setup...

Quit          ⌘Q
```

How Do I Save a File?

To save a file with the current name as shown at the top of the sheet, select FILE, SAVE.

To save a file and give it a new name, use FILE, SAVE AS...

How Do I Delete a File?

Use the FILE, DELETE command. You'll be given your choice of drives. Be careful. Deleted files are gone for good!

How Do I Change Diskettes or Drives?

You must first use one of the other commands to gain access to the drives. You can use FILE, OPEN or FILE, CLOSE or FILE, DE-LETE. Once you have made this selection, Excel will open a directory. You may then select between drives or eject a diskette and replace it with another.

How Do I Close Down?

There are two ways. You can use FILE, CLOSE ALL to close all of the active files. If you've made any changes on any of the files, you will be given an option of saving them. After closing, you will still be in Excel. *Or* you can use the FILE, QUIT command. Again, you will be given the option of saving any changes. However, after all the files have been closed, you will exit Excel.

FORMATTING

How Do I Put Decimals, Dollar Signs, or Time and Date on Values?

First, highlight the range you want formatted. Then use the FOR-MAT, NUMBER command. It will give you options of decimals, dollar signs, or time and date.

How Do I Center Values in a Cell?

Use the FORMAT, ALIGNMENT command. It will allow you to center, put flush left, or put flush right whatever is in a cell.

FIGURE 14–5 Formatting

```
┌─────────────────────────┐
│ Format                  │
│ Number...               │
│ Alignment...            │
│ Style...                │
│ Border...               │
│ Cell Protection...      │
│·························│
│ Column Width...         │
└─────────────────────────┘
```

Can I Use Boldface or Italic?

Yes. Use the FORMAT,STYLE command.

Can I Change the Border of Cells?

First, you must turn off the regular grid display. Use OPTIONS, DISPLAY. Click off GRIDLINES.

Now highlight the cell(s) you want borders on. Use the FORMAT, BORDER command. You are given a variety of options.

How Do I Change the Width of a Column?

The easiest method is to aim the pointer at the border between columns on the column line (the one with letters). When properly aimed, the pointer changes shape. Now drag to right or left as desired.

Alternatively, use FORMAT, WIDTH. You will be given the option of typing the number of characters you'd like to for whatever column happens to be highlighted. (You can change the width of several columns simultaneously by highlighting them and then using this command.)

FORMULAS

How Do I Start a Formula?

For Excel to know that you are entering a formula and not text, labels, or values, you must first use an equal sign [=].

FIGURE 14–6 Formulas

```
┌─────────────────────────┐
│ Formula                 │
│ Paste Name...           │
│ Paste Function...       │
│ Reference          ⌘T   │
│ ·····················   │
│ Define Name...     ⌘L   │
│ Create Names...         │
│ ·····················   │
│ Goto...            ⌘G   │
│ Find...            ⌘H   │
│ Select Last Cell        │
│ Show Active Cell        │
└─────────────────────────┘
```

What Are References?

References are a means of identifying one or more cells. For example, A1 refers to a cell on the worksheet. B2 refers to a different cell. A colon between two references indicates a range. For example, A1:B2 refers to four cells: A1, A2, B1, and B2.

References may be used in formulas. For example, a formula could be written as "=5+3." Or, if the value 5 were in cell A1 and the value 3 in cell B2, it could also be written "=A1+B2."

Excel works geographically. If the above formula were written into cell C1, Excel would understand that it was to add the value in the cell in the same row, but two columns to the left (A1) to that of the value in the cell one row down and one column to the left (B2). It is for this reason that formulas can be filled into whole ranges and still work.

Excel provides an easy way of seeing these relative references, called R1C1. It can be reached from the OPTIONS menu, and it expresses cells in terms of their relative locations. In the above example, cell C1's formula would read "=RC[−2]+R[1]C[−1]." In this format, cells located to the right and down are shown as positive values; those above and to the left are negative. Hence, the description reads: Same row, two columns to the left (RC[−2]) plus one row down, one column to the left (R[1]C[−1]).

What Are Absolute and Relative References?

The references indicated above are all relative; that is, they are a pattern that can be placed anywhere on the worksheet. An absolute reference, however, can only be one cell. For example, A1 is a relative reference. Adding dollar signs, however, changes it to an absolute reference, $A$1. (*Note:* The dollar sign must be added for both the row and the column. Thus it is possible to have part of a reference be absolute and part be relative—for example, A$1. A reference of this kind is called a mixed reference.)

Can I Switch Back and Forth?

The FORMULA, REFERENCE command allows selected references in a formula to be automatically switched among relative, absolute, and mixed references.

What Are Functions?

Functions are a kind of shorthand method of handling complex operations. The simplest function is SUM. For example, we could add all of the values in cells A1:A5 in this fashion: "=A1+A2+A3+A4+A5." Or we could use the SUM function, "=SUM(A1:A5)," and get the same result.

Excel offers dozens of functions. We can get a listing of them under FORMULA, PASTE FUNCTION. (See also the "Functions" section in Chapter 4.) We can also have a selected function pasted into our formula with this command.

What Are Arguments?

Arguments are the information that functions use to perform their task. Arguments are contained within parentheses (). There can be up to seven levels of parentheses in Excel.

Can I Name a Cell, Range, or Formula?

To name, use the FORMULA, DEFINE NAME command. You will be shown a box into which you can write a name. Below the box will be shown the cell or range to which the name refers. Once thus named, this cell or range name can be used in place of the cell reference in formulas.

A group of cells may be named at once using the FORMULA, CREATE NAMES command.

How Do I Find a Named Cell, Range, or Formula?

Use the FORMULA, GOTO command.

Can I Find a Value within a Cell?

Use the FORMULA, FIND command.

MACRO COMMANDS

Excel's macro system is discussed in detail in the "Macros" section of Chapter 4. The following information will be useful as a reminder of what the various commands are.

How Do I Turn On/Off the Recorder?

Be sure you have both a macro sheet and a worksheet active. Be sure you've defined the range to be recorded on the macro sheet using MACRO, SET RECORDER. Use MACRO, START RECORDER to record the macro. This command becomes MACRO, STOP RECORDER and is used to turn the recorder off.

Can I Record Absolute Values on My Macro?

Yes. The normal method is to record relative values. To record absolute values, use MACRO, ABSOLUTE RECORD. To switch back, use the same selection. It becomes MACRO, RELATIVE RECORD.

How Do I Run a Macro?

There are several ways. If you've put a key in the macro, you can key the reference to run it. Or you can select MACRO, RUN.

FIGURE 14–7 Macro Commands

You'll be shown a box containing all of the available macros. Making a selection here will run the appropriate macro.

OTHER QUESTIONS

How Do I Change Active Windows?

The easiest method is to point to any visible part of the window you want active and click. That window will then become active.

If no part of the window you want active is visible, you can use the move bar at the top of the current active window to move it out of the way until you can see the window you desire.

An alternative method is to use WINDOW, NEW WINDOW. This will list all of the current windows. Simply make your selection and it will become active.

Can I Protect a Document or Cells?

Protect cells from being changed by using the FORMAT, CELL PROTECTION command. Lock these cells using the OPTION, PROTECT DOCUMENT command. (*Hint:* Use a familiar term as your password. Otherwise, if you forget the password, you won't be able to get back into your worksheet!)

How Do I Use a Different Font?

Use the OPTION, FONT command. You'll be given a selection of four fonts in a variety of sizes.

FIGURE 14–8 Windows

```
┌─────────────────┐
│ Window          │
├─────────────────┤
│ Show Clipboard  │
│ New Window      │
│.................│
│                 │
│ Budget          │
│ Expenses:1      │
│ Expenses:2      │
│ Mychart         │
└─────────────────┘
```

FIGURE 14–9 Options

```
┌─────────────────────────┐
│ Options                 │
├─────────────────────────┤
│ Set Print Area          │
│ Set Print Titles        │
│ Set Page Break          │
│ Remove Page Break       │
│ ······················· │
│ Font...                 │
│ Display...              │
│ ······················· │
│ Protect Document...     │
│ ······················· │
│ Precision As Displayed  │
│ R1C1                    │
│ Calculate Now      ⌘=   │
│ Calculation...          │
└─────────────────────────┘
```

How Can I Control Calculations?

The OPTION, CALCULATION command instructs Excel to re-calculate the formulas in a document. You can select AUTOMATIC, which recalculates with each change. MANUAL will calculate only when the CALCULATE NOW command is used.

ITERATION will repeat calculations for a set number of times.

The OPTION, PRECISION AS DISPLAYED command instructs Excel to calculate on the basis of values as displayed, not as carried out to 14 digits, which is the usual procedure.

Index